An Altar Boy's Confession

*How This Street-Smart Kid from
Brooklyn Became a Suburban
Mamaluke**

By Rich Sfraga

Norah Global Media

ISBN: 978-1-962957-15-1 (Ebook)

ISBN: 978-1-962957-16-8 (Paperback)

ISBN: 978-1-962957-17-5 (Audiobook)

Norah Global Media, LLC

https://www.norahmedia.com/

4520 East West Highway, Suite 780

Bethesda, MD 20814

This memoir is dedicated to my wife, Lisa, my personal lifesaver, therapist, and occasional voice of reason. From the moment we met, we both recognized something special, knowing we were worth saving. She's stood by me through thick and thin, surviving my bad jokes, questionable decisions, and occasional bouts of sheer stubbornness. Without her, I'd probably still be wandering aimlessly, so really, this book is as much hers as it is mine.

I also dedicate this book to my three sons, who have grown into men far better than I could ever hope to be. Our relationship has evolved from father and sons to something even greater—"almost" best friends. They inspire me to do better each day simply because they do better each day. This book is also for them, so they can see the mistakes I've made and, knowing the incredible men they've become, I have no doubt they'll never repeat them. They are great human beings, and I couldn't be prouder.

Disclaimer

This memoir is a work of personal recollection and reflection. The events, conversations, and individuals depicted are based on the author's memories and perspectives. Some names, identifying details, and sequences of events have been altered, condensed, or reconstructed for narrative coherence and to respect privacy. Any resemblance to actual persons, living or deceased, beyond those explicitly identified, is purely coincidental.

The opinions expressed are solely those of the author and do not reflect the views of any organization, institution, or entity. This book is not intended as a definitive historical account but rather as the author's subjective experience. The author and publisher make no claims, promises, or guarantees regarding the accuracy, completeness, or reliability of the information presented.

The content of this book is provided "as is," without warranties of any kind, express or implied. The author and publisher disclaim any liability for any loss, damage, or inconvenience resulting from its use.

Readers are encouraged to remember that memory is fallible, perspectives evolve, and personal experiences may differ.

So... What's a Mamaluke?

*Mamaluke (mama-LOO-keh):** A Mamaluke is an Italian slang term for someone who does something dumb, stupid, silly, or foolish, or someone who is dumb, stupid, silly, or foolish.

I thought being street-smart meant I'd never get played. I knew how to read people, spot a scam, and talk my way out of trouble. So, how did I end up making mistakes as an adult that I should've seen coming a mile away?

Growing up in Bensonhurst, Brooklyn, I learned how to survive—whether it was in Catholic school, fist fights left and right, or brushing shoulders with wise guys. But nothing prepared me for the struggles that came later. When bad decisions caught up with me, I was forced to face something I never had before: the consequences. The mental wildfire of regret, self-doubt, and trying to fix what I broke nearly consumed me. But in the end, it wasn't my street smarts that saved me—it was the love and loyalty of my wife and kids.

An Altar Boy's Confession is a raw, funny, and heartfelt memoir about growing up Italian American in Brooklyn, learning lessons the hard way, and discovering that sometimes, the toughest battles aren't on the streets—they're in your own mind.

Rich Sfraga, a Brooklyn native and storyteller, is a proud husband, father, and grandfather—living life like a boss. As for his future destiny? You'll find him in the woods, tracking down his golf ball on the course.

Table of Contents

Preface

I've been tossing snapshots of my life around for as long as I can remember. Every time I share one of these stories, people either end up in stitches, laughing until it hurts, or they're so moved it brings them to tears. And sure, some people don't believe half the tales I tell—not until my friends jump in, backing me up word for word. That's when they realize, "Yeah, this wild stuff actually happened."

Now, I know I was an altar boy as a kid, and not all my choices have exactly screamed "altar boy lifestyle." But I'm not some delinquent; I'm just a guy who had a lot of tough situations come my way and had to claw my way through them. And I did exactly that. Every story here, every twist and turn has a silver lining—even if it's a little rough around the edges. Because the truth is, no matter how bad things got, they could've been a hell of a lot worse.

Beyond just sharing these stories, I hope to reach people who feel trapped, stuck in some nightmare situation, thinking there's no way out. If this book can show them that I imperfectly stumbled my way to the other side, they'll feel a glimmer of hope. They'll realize that even in the darkest moments, there's a way forward—even if it's messy, even if it's flawed, it's there.

Also, I wanted to put these stories together so family and friends could see where my head was through all of this and really understand the mindset I had in those moments. And, yeah, I'll admit, dredging up some of these memories wasn't easy. There were some stories I couldn't even put into words until years after they'd happened, and it felt like ripping off a friggin' scab to write them down. But it was cathartic, too. Like an exorcism—hard as hell, but worth every second.

I didn't hold back on the language, either. This is written the way I grew up talking—the rough, real, no-bullshit language of Brooklyn. It's blunt, it's profane, it's the slang that's as much a part of me as my own skin. This is me, unfiltered, raw, and real. So, buckle up.

Chapter 1

I Should've Known I Was Fucked

My alleged business partner, John Rizzo, called and asked me to meet him at a potential new client's office in Princeton, New Jersey. Rizzo was a bit older than I and a Michael J. Fox look-a-like but wasn't as endearing as his movie characters. He was an arrogant and smug person who rubbed people the wrong way. He wore a ton of cologne that I can still smell wafting through the air years later.

Rizzo was in finance before we got into business and at the time, it seemed like a good idea to partner with someone who knew the financial side of things. I put his personality aside and dealt with his bullshit because math wasn't my thing. He had no background in construction engineering, despite it being our field. By then, I had been working in engineering for a few years, building contacts, so I found it odd that he was bringing in new business when that was my job. Most of our business was in New York City, where the rules are the strictest in the country. I came to realize during my

association with Rizzo that he was good at one thing—
he knew how to fucking scam people and I naively was
becoming his latest victim.

That day in Princeton, he stood strangely in the
light rain outside a nondescript office building. He was
rushing me inside, and he seemed uptight and quiet.
Naturally, he made no mention that the new client was
just a ruse to get me to attend this meeting. We entered
the office, but nobody was in the room yet. It was an
amazing space, filled with New York Giants and
Yankees memorabilia. It looked like a museum that had
autographed jerseys along with plaques hung on the
walls. A giant image of Derek Jeter made it feel like he
might peel off the wall and step into the office to say
hello!

As we sat down in front of the empty desk, I asked
Rizzo whose office this was. He said it was Ed
Lombardo's office. I was taken aback by his answer
because Lombardo was a guy who we sold our accounts
receivables to and not a new client! We were short on
cash, so Lombardo gave us the full amount of our
outstanding invoices upfront. When the client paid us,
Lombardo took his 3% fee. Everything was legal with
signed contracts! It was a win-win, until today—when
the shit hit the fan.

Just as I was asking what the hell we were doing at Lombardo's office, Ed came walking in. He was a pretty fat dude who wore expensive suits two times too small. I never understand guys who waste all that cash on suits that don't fit. If you can afford the expensive clothes, then get a tailor to fit the suit over your fat ass.

Ed bypassed all the usual pleasantries of a business meeting and got right to the point. He said to me, "You know, Rich, when people owe me a half million dollars and aren't paying me back, I get fuckin' pissed!"

I lost all oxygen to my brain as I looked at Rizzo because just a week prior, he had told me we only owed Lombardo forty thousand dollars from our receivables, and we were up to date. The feeling of distrust was overwhelming, as Rizzo sat stone-faced, like he set me up for this.

So then, this fuckin' guy goes behind his desk and takes out a Paul O'Neill-signed baseball bat. As he taps the bat in his hand, he comes behind me and says, "Do you know what I do to people who owe me that kind a money?"

I thought that this was a good time to cool down the situation and make a joke, like, *this isn't the first time someone threatened me with a bat*, but I had no spit to even speak.

He gets into his home run stance and smashes the bat across the back of my chair. The pop rang through my ears and the force of the blow felt as if I was rear-ended by a horse. I was fucking scared shitless but couldn't show it. I went through some crazy stuff in my life and was lucky to come out alive, but I was getting too old for this shit. I would've agreed to anything he wanted at this point.

After Slugger broke the bat against the chair instead of my head, he nonchalantly began to explain to me that he and his brother, who were financial advisors, were in a lot of trouble. They were running a Ponzi scheme with the funds they were lending us. He didn't exactly use the words Ponzi or scheme, but there was no need for him to mince words. The brothers told clients their investments were going into real estate, but in fact that money was going to fund our companies' receivables. Their plan exploded when the stock market crashed, and the duped clients were looking for their money and would-be profits.

Rizzo calmly turned to me and said, "I've already come up with a plan to pay Ed back, so he doesn't have to go to prison. We front him $100k and continue to pay him $5000 a week until he's paid off."

The problem with this plan is that Rizzo and I can't get paid for a while because it's such a big nut. This was the point where I felt paralyzed and began to bury my head in the sand. I should have run out of that office screaming for my mommy, but I had so much of me invested in this venture. Now we owed a boat load of cash to this crooked, crazy bastard.

How am I going to survive with nothing coming in? Wild, right? This is just the tip of the iceberg in my life. I'd been in tight spots before—some terrifying, some downright funny. Looking back, it's wild to see how things spiraled out of control, yet somehow, I always managed to land on my feet—and all the while, I can see I was a fortunate guy at the same time.

Chapter 2

Little Richie Shenanigans

Let me delve into some of those fucked up situations and take you back to where it all began—Bensonhurst, Brooklyn, and especially, 80th Street and 18th Avenue, the cross streets I lived on. Bensonhurst during the '70s and '80s meant living in a neighborhood where the mob's presence was impossible to ignore. Everyone seemed to know someone connected to the Italian mob, and it shaped the rhythm of the streets. Crime against residents was rare—mobsters focused on their own business—so people joked that they kept the neighborhood safe. Social clubs and small businesses were often rumored to have mob connections, but it was all part of the backdrop of everyday life.

Walking around streets like 18th Ave, 13th Ave, or 86th St was a daily routine. The air was filled with the mouthwatering aroma of Italian food—freshly baked bread, sausage and peppers, and roasted garlic from the salumerias and pizzerias. I'd grab a loaf of bread and couldn't resist tearing off the end to eat on the walk home. It was a place where there was a true sense of community.

My parents weren't involved at all with the mafia, but they knew how to keep us safe in that crazy environment. They were hardworking, middle-class Italians who just wanted the best for me and my sister. Simple dreams, you know? A good education, a decent income, and the experience of Italian traditions that the neighborhood had to offer.

My dad worked as a printer in Rockefeller Center; his office faced the ice-skating rink with the huge Christmas tree. At every tree lighting ceremony, my mom would take me and my sister on the train to his office for the big event, and just before the lighting, I'd flick the light switches on and off, thinking I'd show up on TV. Instead, I'm sure I annoyed everyone in my father's office!

He always dressed in slacks, a dress shirt, and a tie, even on weekends—minus the tie. It always confused me as a kid because he never wore a tracksuit or jeans like the other dads. He had his own sense of style, I guess. He wasn't the conventional father figure who dished out profound life lessons or sage advice. Instead, he was the dad who made weekends memorable, the one who would play catch with me in the driveway of our apartment.

He introduced me to the forgotten art of boxball (if you're curious, give it a quick Google search, you lazy bastards). We hopped over to the local playground in Dyker Beach Park on weekends, where we would play ball, or once, we carved our initials into a tree. Those initials were there every time I passed that tree for years! Usually, we hung out while our paisans engaged in a lively (to put it mildly) game of Bocci. Those guys would scream in Italian at each other like somebody stole a meatball off their dinner plate! But our special bonding moments were often found on the golf course.

Golf was an unexpected pastime for an Italian kid in those days. It was considered a game for old men since, in my neighborhood, baseball, football, basketball, and hockey reigned supreme. Yet, my dad and I defied convention. He may not have been a fountain of wisdom, but I'll never forget his simple words during a round of golf at Dyker Beach Golf Course.

After a particularly bad outing, he pointed to a golfer ahead of us who completely whiffed at the ball on the tee. He said to me, "Look at that guy, Rich. There's always someone having a worse day than you." I internalized that advice, applying it to many circumstances throughout my life.

Simple, but it hit home. That piece of advice followed me through a lot of bad days since then.

Whether I was in a jam, or things weren't going my way, I'd remember my father's words, and somehow it always made me feel just a little better. Even in the middle of all the chaos, it was a reminder that someone else out there was getting screwed worse than I was.

My father was a staunch believer in dedicating yourself to a company until the day the pallbearers escorted your casket into the hearse. He may not have approved of some of my decisions, but I believe his disapproval stemmed from worry, concern, and perhaps ridiculous fears that I would turn gay or something.

My mom, on the other hand, assumed the role of housewife and financial planner. She took care of everything and managed the money like a pro, stretching every dollar like nobody's business. I remember her going to a store on 13th Avenue, buying a couple of yards of gray fabric, a zipper, blue striping, and a pattern for boys' pants. She then sewed my school uniform together from that pile of stuff. But no matter how hard she tried, the fucking navy stripe on the side always came apart by the end of the year. I remember all my friends having these cool, flared pants that made them look like they just got off the dance floor... and then there's me, tripping over my navy stripe as it dangled on the floor.

My mother did a lot for us, but I'm not sure she was ever happy with how her life turned out. Before she met my father, she had contemplated a life as a nun, and honestly, there was something about her that made me feel like she belonged in that life.

While I was growing up, their relationship was filled with silence. They constantly fought and he gave her the silent treatment. As a kid, it was deafening. They didn't talk to each other that much, and that emptiness was hard to ignore. My mom tried to live out her missed dreams through us, pushing us to do things she never got to experience. She made sure we got into the best schools and always pushed us to try new things. I could tell she was living her life through our accomplishments, trying to find happiness she didn't get growing up. Her childhood wasn't easy because it was full of sadness and struggle. Now, as I look back, I understand her a lot more and empathize with her past.

While my parents did their best to provide us with opportunities they never had, there was a definite childhood memory that still has me cracking up, forever etched in my mind like a fucking sitcom. We lived in the rear apartment of a three-family house, and as a young kid, the place seemed fucking huge. Now, keep in mind, I was just a tiny human with a wild imagination, so everything felt larger than life.

One afternoon, when I was about 4 years old, my mom was out in the hallway, having a classic bullshitting session with our neighbor from the front apartment. Meanwhile, I was inside, playing with my GI Joe. I had "Buggs Bunny" on TV and jumped from one couch to another like a maniac. Somewhere in between bouncing around and laughing, I got my hands on a Charms lollipop—a sucker that was way too big for my little mouth. But, of course, at four, you think you're invincible. I shoved the whole thing in, taking in the deliciousness.

Then, catastrophe struck. I pulled the lollipop out, and only the stick was left! The fucking thing slipped down my throat, and I stood there, not even realizing I was about to choke to death. I strolled into the hallway, holding the empty stick like I'd just pulled off some magic trick, totally unaware that I was in deep trouble.

The second my mom and the neighbor laid eyes on me, their faces turned pale. I'm sure I looked like a purple eggplant, not breathing, with that friggin' lollipop jammed in my throat. My mom dropped her cigarette on the floor and screamed louder than anything out of a horror movie.

The neighbor's eyes nearly popped out of her sockets. And faster than you can say "gag reflex," she came to the rescue, grabbing me by the ankles, and flipping me upside down like I was some human piñata. There I was, dangling, seeing the world upside down when she started shaking me. Next thing I knew, the lollipop shot out of my mouth and flew across the hallway.

I was scared out of my mind and didn't know what was happening. But once I started breathing again, all I could think was how cool the neighbor was—she was like a rock star. My mom, on the other hand, got an earful from my dad later. He was pissed that she'd given me the lollipop in the first place.

From that day on, every time I see a lollipop, I can't help but remember that moment. This was an event that felt frozen in time. As I was dangling upside down—breathless, and shaken violently—I knew at age four that my life wouldn't be a piece of cake.

"RICHIE!!! ... RICHIE!!! ... RICHIE!!" That was the sound that pierced my eardrums every single morning, courtesy of my best friend Aldo and his annoying sister Carmella. Aldo always had his tongue perpetually hanging out like a drooling dog, and Carmella was a pint-sized bundle of mischief. They screamed my name, simultaneously, like they were auditioning for the madcap choir. I swear, they wouldn't shut the fuck up until I finally came out of the house. Now, my mother had her own set of rules, insisting that I needed to shower before embarking on any grand adventures with the brother and sister duo. So, there I was, trapped in the bathroom, contemplating whether hygiene was worth the deafening screams from across the street.

Don't get me wrong, they were nice kids to hang out with—Aldo was my pal and Carmella, well, she was cool when she wasn't driving me nuts—but they weren't exactly what you'd call exciting. In fact, most days they were about as thrilling as watching paint dry. That is, until the day we decided to play KARATE.

I don't know what got into us, too many Bruce Lee movies or Saturday morning cartoons, but we were out there, acting like we were martial arts masters. Aldo was doing some goofy karate chops, and I was showing off my best kick when Carmella, out of nowhere, decided she was the next Karate Kid. And let me tell you, she didn't hold back. With all the power in her tiny legs, she kicked me right in the balls.

The pain took over my body. One second, I was standing; the next, I was on the pavement, clutching my balls and praying a comet would come screaming to earth to end the agony. It was like someone had ripped my soul out through my... well, you get the point. My eyes shot open, my voice hit notes I didn't even know I could reach, and the world turned into a blur of agony. And where was Aldo during all this? My bestie was standing there, frozen for a second before going into full panic mode.

"Francis! Francis!" Aldo starts yelling like the town crier for my mom, "Richie got kicked in the balls and he's lying on the street!!"

Now, if you thought my day couldn't get worse, you'd be dead wrong. Because the next thing I know, my mother comes charging out of the house like some kind of superhero. And what does she do? Does she calmly check on me? No. She pulls my pants down right there, in front of all my friends and neighbors, to "assess the damage," as she called it. I'm telling you, I could've died right then and there.

And, of course, just my luck—my poor apples had swollen to the size of, well, actual apples. Not the small ones either. I'm talking about those giant ones you pick out at the grocery store, the ones that are so big they barely fit in your hand.

As I lay there, pants down, pride shattered, all I could think about was how much I wished the earth would open up and swallow me whole. But nope, I had to endure the humiliation of my mother inspecting me like I was a school science project.

Who would've thought that an apple could mess with a grown man's head so much? But let me take you back to the good old' days, when fruit was just a side dish, and block parties in Bensonhurst were where the real action was. I'm talking about the street being packed with people, food everywhere, music blasting, and kids running around like they'd just discovered sugar.

Every summer, the whole street would close off to traffic, and—BAM!—instant party. Folding tables full of food lined up on the sidewalk—Italian dishes that would make your grandma cry and BBQ that had your mouth watering from two blocks away. You couldn't walk ten feet without smelling sausages, burgers, or something sizzling away. And then there were the kids, hyped up and zooming around in their own little world. The DJ? Fuhgeddaboudit. They had people shaking their asses like there was no tomorrow. Carnival rides, games, you name it—those block parties had it all. For a few hours, life was perfect—no worries, just pure fun.

One year, they decided to have a bicycle race, and of course, I signed up. I was so pumped, thinking I'd finally get a win under my belt. I was ready, my bike looked good, and I felt good. And then the race started.

"READY, SET, GO!" one of the dads shouted, and I took off like a bat outta hell, peddling as fast as I could. But no sooner had I hit my stride when—CRACK! My handlebars snapped right off the bike! I didn't know whether to scream or laugh. But what happened next was no joke because the sharp metal cut right through my shorts and sliced into my—you got it—my balls.

Next thing I know, I'm laid out on the pavement, bleeding like a stuffed pig from where no man should ever bleed. And just like before, my mom came running over, this time with gauze and bandages. Right there in front of the whole block, she pulled down my shorts to clean me up. There I was again, my balls hanging out for all to see, and Stevie Wonder's "Superstition" playing in the background like a soundtrack to my misery.

How was I supposed to show my face after that? Exposed, humiliated, and in pain—again. I spent the rest of that block party sitting on my front stoop, refusing to leave for fear of anyone pointing and laughing.

But you know, the funny part is, this wasn't even the first humiliating thing that happened to me that day. Earlier that morning, I ran alongside the street sweeper—don't ask me why, I thought it was fun—getting soaked by the mist it kicked up. Only, it wasn't mist. It was filthy water and dirt. So yeah, I spent the first half of the day looking like a drowned sewer rat.

But still, even with all the bruises, blood, and humiliation, those block parties were something special. It's crazy how no matter how many times you get knocked down, you still find a way to laugh about it later. Trust me though, this isn't the last time you'll hear about my poor, battered private parts!

I went to a Catholic grammar school on 71st St and 15th Ave. Every day, I walked over a mile to school, and my parents didn't worry much. Back then, it was the kind of neighborhood where people looked out for each other. Well, except for me. I always had to watch my own ass.

On my way home, I'd pass by the candy store on New Utrecht Avenue to grab a snack. It was my usual stop. But one afternoon, there was a dead body right in the doorway. Yep, no candy for me that day. My mom, trying to shield me like she always did, told me the guy choked on pancakes. But the blood spilling into the street told a different story. I figured he didn't make it inside for any pancakes, or he just took them to-go, you know?

But that was just one type of challenge I faced every day in the neighborhood. The real trouble came from the Bosso brothers—the biggest bullies in Bensonhurst. These two lived in an apartment building right on my corner, and they had a routine. Every day after school, knowing I'd have to pass by, they'd wait for me, hiding in the alley like a couple of lions waiting to pounce— and pounce they did. One would hold me down while the other beat the crap out of me. I was their personal punching bag.

You'd think I'd be smart enough to take the long way home, right? But hell, no. That would mean they won, and there was no way I was letting those assholes think they had me scared. So, every day, I walked right past their building and took my beating like a champ. What my parents didn't know was their son was going twelve rounds with Randy Savage and Hulk Hogan every day after school.

One day, though, the secret was out. This old Italian guy from down the street came over, rang our doorbell, and introduced himself to my mom. He had this thick accent, and he said, "You should be proud of your son. Every day, the Bosso brothers gang up on him, but he irritates them because he keeps getting his own shots in." My mom's jaw dropped. She had no idea her kid was out there fighting his own WWF matches in the middle of the street.

Eventually, the Bosso brothers got bored with me, I guess. They moved on to bigger and worse things. Years later, one of them, who thought he was going to a meeting to become a *made man*, got shot in the head and was found slumped over in his Camaro, and the other one? He ended up behind bars, locked up for God knows what. But those brothers are a whole other story.

So yeah, walking to school wasn't just about dodging traffic; it was about dodging fists, dead bodies, and neighborhood drama. But somehow, through all that, I survived. Brooklyn's got a funny way of teaching you to toughen up.

Using my fists and street smarts became part of my daily survival in the neighborhood. It was like there were assassins around every corner, just waiting for the perfect moment to jump me. Within a block or two of my house, I always felt like someone was ready to test me, keeping me on high alert.

One summer night, I was sent to grab a pizza for dinner from 18th Avenue. Simple task, right? But nothing's ever simple in my world. I was on the corner of 18th Avenue and 81st Street, waving to each store owner as I passed by, the smell of that pizza making my mouth water. I couldn't wait to dig in. But then, just as I had the box in my hand, two little shits popped out of nowhere, determined to take that pizza for themselves.

I wasn't in the mood for this. I told them, "Leave me the fuck alone or I'll bash you in the fucking face!"

Normally, that would have been enough to scare off most punks. But not these two. They were dead set on taking that pizza from me. What followed was like a tug of war with me on one side, the pizza box in the middle, and these two goons trying to rip it from my hands.

People were just passing by like it was some regular day, not even batting an eye, while I was out there fighting for my life—or more accurately, for my pizza. I didn't care what happened to me at that point. All I cared about was getting the pizza home. If I showed up without it, I knew my dad would be pissed.

After what felt like forever, I finally managed to break free from those two idiots, still clutching the pizza like it was sacred treasure. I thought I'd actually pulled it off. But when I got home and opened the box, I realized the battle wasn't without its casualties. The pizza looked like it had been through the Tomatina Festival—sauce and cheese everywhere. My parents, especially my dad, got pissed and asked what the hell happened. I couldn't exactly tell them I got into a fight over the pizza, so I just said, "I walked into a pole." Knowing me, they bought it. They always thought I wasn't paying attention.

That was the thing about me. I was always trying to protect people, even if they didn't care about me or did me wrong. I never learned from my mistakes. I just kept rolling with the punches, both figuratively and literally. That pizza fight didn't make me more cautious—it just made me more determined. Every time I step into a pizzeria now, I remember that night. No matter what, I'll always fight to get the pizza home.

When the weather got nice, I loved riding my bike around the block. It felt like freedom, even though I had to stick to the sidewalk and just rode in circles. There was this building on 79th Street with these kids who always hung out in packs. They were bad news, like a bunch of wolves just waiting for something to happen. Every time I passed, I rode as fast as I could because I knew better than to slow down around them.

One day, I made the mistake of dropping my guard. Sure enough, this greasy little punk in a dirty Ginny tee steps out in front of my bike and grabs the handlebars. He had snot hanging out of his nose and, in the most disgusting voice, told me to get off my bike because he wanted it. I didn't even think twice. I just punched him right in the face. The snot turned blood red, and I took off, crying down the street—still on my bike, by the way.

Why was I crying? I didn't do anything wrong, but for some reason, I still felt bad. It's because, deep down, I didn't want to hurt anyone, not even a kid like him. But after that day, I never rode my bike down his block again. That one bloody punch changed everything.

The cross street of my block was New Utrecht Avenue, with its elevated train tracks overhead. The station was just a block away on 79th Street. In the winter, these massive icicles would hang from the underside of the train station—huge, some about a foot thick and five feet long. You couldn't walk past them without thinking what would happen if they fell.

It was a winter afternoon, the sun shining bright, warming things up just enough for the icicles to start dripping onto the street. Me and my friend, Joe Mazza, were out there under the station, having a contest to see who could knock one of them down with a snowball. We kept missing, getting frustrated, but I wasn't about to let that stop me. I made the perfect snowballa mix of slush and snow, just the right weight.

I wound up and threw it with all my might, aiming high. BAM! It hit the top of the icicle dead-on. What happened next was like something out of a movie. The icicle came crashing down, piercing right through the roof of a yellow Chevy station wagon parked below. You could hear the gasps from the people around us. Some even ran into the candy store nearby to avoid getting blamed for it.

I just stood there for a second, watching in shock at the total destruction I'd caused, and without thinking, I took off running. I didn't stop until I was far enough away to feel safe. I had no clue where I was and had to check the street signs to get my bearings. Joey? He ran the other way, and when I finally saw him again weeks later, we didn't even mention what happened.

I never went back to that candy store, too paranoid the owner had figured it out. And as for the car owner? I wasn't stupid enough to stick around to find out how they reacted. No one ever found out it was me, so there were no repercussions. Sure, I felt guilty at first, but after a while, I started telling the story to my friends, and we'd all get a good laugh out of it. Weird thing was, after that, some of the kids even looked up to me. That one event somehow turned into a cool story that gave me a little street cred.

Like I said earlier, our apartment was in the back of the house, on the second floor. From the rear windows, you could see into the backyards of the houses on the next street over. We had a clothesline out the window, and one of my regular chores was to hang wet clothes out there. You can imagine that it gets real boring after a while.

So, I started finding other ways to amuse myself out of that window. (Get your mind out of the gutter! I wasn't flashing the neighbors, you perverts!) Anyway, one day I went into the junk drawer and grabbed a book of matches. I'd seen my parents light them a million times, so I figured, how hard could it be?

I struck the first match and burnt my friggin' finger because who knew you had to move your finger? But I wasn't about to give up. I struck another one—and burnt another finger. The next time, I got the hang of it, but as soon as I started lighting them, some nosy lady from her back window spotted me and started screaming across the yard, saying she was going to come around the block and tell my mother I was playing with matches! I was petrified.

I dropped the matches, ran to the sink, and stuck my burnt fingers under the cold water. I waited around like a fool for months, thinking that any day that lady would come banging on our door to rat me out. I always gave my mother a lame excuse for why I didn't want to hang the clothes out the window any longer. I didn't go near that back window for the longest time.

You would think playing in the front of the house would be safer, but that's the first time I got hit by a car—yeah, the first time. It was one of those sweltering July days when everyone in Bensonhurst was outside, soaking up the summer because no one had air conditioning back then. About eight of us were playing tag on our bikes. We'd be racing through alleys, hopping curbs, and darting into the street without a second thought for any oncoming cars. My neighbor across the street, Mr. "I-Love-My-Chevy" Impala, washed that car more than anyone I've ever seen. It was his pride and joy, and if we so much as looked at it while playing ball, he'd yell at us not to even think about touching it.

So, there I was, flying down the street, trying to tag Bobby Russo, when wouldn't you know it, this guy decides to cruise down the block in his precious Impala. I raced out into the street, and—BANG—I smacked right into his car. Time felt like it stood still as I saw the car right in front of me. My handlebar got stuck in the grill and I got up, limping around. He jumped out and started screaming like I'd killed his firstborn. Not once did he ask me if I was hurt. Nah, all he cared about was his friggin' car. I didn't say a word. I just ditched the bike and took off running home, knowing my mom would freak out if she found out what happened.

Did I actually think this guy wouldn't follow me to my house? I was upstairs bawling, my mom having no idea what the hell was wrong with me, when the doorbell rang. It was him, still screaming about his precious car—and holding my bike. I was expecting at least, "Are you alright, kid?" Nope. All I got was more yelling about his car. My mom made me go downstairs and apologize to him. That was the last thing I wanted to do, but I did it anyway.

Physically, I was okay except for a slight limp, but emotionally, I was a mess. The moment I got hit, I felt this rush of fear. I always dreaded passing that guy's house after that, half-expecting him to jump out at me like a boogeyman. It felt like the entire block witnessed the whole scene. One woman even shouted in her thick Italian accent, "I knew one of them little bastards was gonna get hit one day!"

Despite the punishment I faced at home for being a dick, I got right back on my bike a few days later. You know what they say: "Get right back up on the horse after you fall off." But honestly, I wasn't afraid to ride again. It was that naive childhood bravado, or maybe I just loved the thrill too much.

After that, I added his house to my growing list of places I had to avoid. Between that and the other situations I managed to be involved in, I was running out of spots to hang around in my own neighborhood. Thank God I was getting old enough to venture further out, places where people didn't know me or my ballinas. But let's be real, knowing me, I'd find a way to cause a commotion somewhere else. And trust me, I did. My story's far from over.

Chapter 3

Our Lady of Holy Terror School

When I wasn't dodging punches or stepping over a dead body on the way to school, I had a memorable time as a student and altar boy at Our Lady of Guadalupe. OLG was your typical Catholic school in the 1970s, complete with its own set of nuns who ruled the place with an iron fist.

Well, they usually didn't use their fists. Each had their weapon of choice. The principal, Sister Filomena, walked around with a paddle, practically licking her chops, ready to use it on a tiny tush. Sister Ann took your measurements with a yardstick, and when she was done, the numbers were embossed on your knuckles. Sister Rose had her umbrella—you'd pray for rain so she'd need it for its original purpose, but otherwise, she'd smash you upside the head with it. Meanwhile, Sister Christina had pinpoint accuracy with her pointer stick—she could whack you between your collar and hairline with marksmanship precision.

Not only did I stress about wearing my home made school uniform, but I also had to deal with these prescription shoes—yes, prescription shoes! I was a bit pigeon-toed. The doctor thought it was necessary to sap my self-esteem by telling my mom that these shoes would fix me right up. Can you believe that? I ended up looking like Herman Munster decided to go back to elementary school. Those shoes were disgusting! They were big, bulky, and uglier than sin itself.

And you won't believe the nonsense I had to hear from my mom about these shoes. All she talked about was how they were made of genuine leather and how all my friends had fake shoes. Fake shoes? Come on, now! To me, their shoes looked pretty cool. They caught the eye of all the girls in class—or at least I thought so. But you know who mine probably caught the eye of? Herman's wife, Lily.

But wait, it wasn't just the outfit and shoes. It was my snow boots too. While all the other boys were rocking these slick slip-on boots, I had to wear boots that felt like they had a hundred clips on them. I dreaded snowstorms back then because I knew I'd get taunted relentlessly in school with those clunky boots of mine. My parents' taste in footwear just didn't cut it.

I thought I was in the clear when some kid in class took a knife and cut all those buckles off the boots. I was like, "Yay, now I'm free!" But guess what? My mom had Joey's mother pay for a new pair of boots, and the agony continued. Talk about bad luck.

Looking back, I gotta admit, it was all in my head. Maybe the other kids didn't even notice my attire or care about my shoes. Who knows!

I didn't get into any real trouble in the school itself. Although, anything I did do might be erased from my memory. For some reason, my classmates were a bad bunch and always in trouble. My fourth-grade class was the pinnacle of madness at OLG.

One of the boys came up with a game that haunts me to this day. Even now, writing about it makes me cringe and hide my privates. He called it *The Electrocution*! He would go around to the boys or the girls, grab their crotch, and yell, "ELECTROCUTION!" He wouldn't let go and squeezed as hard as he could. Soon, other boys started doing it too. It took over the class like a tidal wave. I think most of them were doing it so they wouldn't be the victim. I was scared shitless because it really hurt, and at 10 years old, you have no idea what the fuck is going on.

Forget about gym class—it was the worst. Everyone would be changing, and here he comes, like a buzzsaw, mowing down each kid in class while they had their shorts on. Some of the girls complained to the teachers, but the boys were too humiliated to bring it up.

The nuns found out, and they had no idea what to do. They didn't want to let the parents know what was going on. Back then, it was a different world, and they didn't bring stuff like that up. So, what did they do? Naturally, when in doubt, cover it up and punish the whole class. We had to write in our notebooks about a thousand times something like *I WILL OBEY MY TEACHERS AT ALL TIMES*. You can bet that taught us a lesson. God forbid you go to the parents with a problem like that! I guess they had enough sexual stuff to contend with back then.

When I was an altar boy, I had an easy way out of class because I had to perform funerals sometimes, and I was ecstatic. How could I be so happy going to a funeral? Did you read the first sentence of this paragraph? After the funerals, I would walk back slowly to the school to savor the last few moments of missing class. It was a great feeling getting up in the middle of class to tell the teacher I had to go to Mass. It was truly my get-out-of-jail-free card.

But the absolute best part about being an altar boy was performing the weddings—all that pomp and circumstance, the beauty of the sacrament, the hot bridesmaids, and the tip from the best man—ahhh...

I remember my first wedding. I was ten years old and nervous as heck. Now, I don't want to curse during this part of the story because it has to do with the church and all, so bear with me.

The church was packed with the bride and groom's family and friends. Naturally, my mother was in the last pew to witness my first wedding. Not only was I nervous, but I had to pee so badly. I was physically shaking like a leaf while I waited for the bride to walk down the aisle. The groom romantically takes the bride up the altar steps and kneels in front of the priest.

I'm ready with the rings that are to be blessed, but I had the hardest time keeping the gold tray from shaking. At that moment, I could feel some tingling under my vestments. I wasn't paying attention to the words the priest was saying anymore. I had to concentrate on holding in my urine. I figured I was okay because I had all those clothes on to hide the little bit of pee that might have escaped.

The groom suddenly has a wide smile on his face and nudges the bride, who's all dressed in white. They both look at me, then at the marble floor beneath my feet, and burst out laughing. I had peed on God's altar!! I was standing there in front of hundreds of people in a puddle of my own urine. I was mortified, but what could I do? I had to wait out the ceremony and get back to the sacristy where I could change. After it was over, the best man came back to see me and handed me a $50 bill. He chuckled and said he used to be an altar boy and knew the feeling of performing a wedding.

Hmmm... fifty bucks was a major score for a ten-year-old kid back in the day. My mother chastised me the whole way home, but I gotta admit, I felt pretty good about myself with that extra cash in my pocket. What was the question I had to ask myself? How can I make that much money at the next wedding?

The priests never bothered me back then. They never hit me and never hit on me. Even though I'm straight, should I have been offended that I wasn't an object of their affection? I mean, what was wrong with me? Anyway...

Father George was one of the parish priests back then. He was a funny, burly man who gave great sermons. Unfortunately, he might have given a bad sermon to a male prostitute under the Brooklyn Bridge because they found Father Fred stabbed to death. They washed that story under the bridge... (Get it? Brooklyn Bridge? Washed the story?? Eh... forget it!)

Back then, the priests would come into our classroom and try to convince the boys that we might hear God "calling" us to the priesthood. It sounded like a pretty good deal to me for a few seconds. Here, you have a free place to live, not much work, people look up to you, and even a free car. I weighed the options for a moment, and I thought to myself, "What about the no-sex part?" I quickly came up with, I'd rather live in a house, working hard never hurt anybody, I'm short so people are going to be looking down at me anyway, and priests drive crappy cars.

Chapter 4

All in the Staten Island Family

Most weekends, we'd pile into the Chevy and head to my aunt's place on Staten Island, crossing over from Brooklyn with all the windows down to feel the summer air rolling through. Driving over the Verrazzano Narrows Bridge, I'd glance out the window, catching sight of Fort Wadsworth and imagining soldiers standing guard, as they once did, protecting New York Harbor for two centuries. Further along, my gaze would drift to the hills rising along the expressway, where huge mansions perched like pieces in a giant's Lego set. I'd picture life up there—a sweeping view of the skyline, the harbor, and the hoity-toity stories shared only with those fortunate enough to call that place home.

For a Brooklyn kid in the '70s, the island was like another world, just enough removed from the city's bustle to feel wide-open and wild, like you could run all day and never reach an end. My aunt and uncle, like a lot of Italian Brooklynites back then, had packed up and moved across the Narrows. Their house sat at the end of a quiet street, which felt like paradise to me. The house was a large High Ranch, a familiar sight in Staten Island, yet impressive all the same. The kitchen was enormous and had an island, which was a rare luxury in homes back then. Compared to the Brooklyn homes I knew, this place felt fuckin' huge, its size and layout a big change from what I was accustomed to.

My cousins, a whole pack of older kids, were heroes in my eyes, and I just loved being there with them. When I got older, I'd hear stories about the two youngest, Anthony and Vincent, from people who knew them around Staten Island. They seemed to have blazed their own trail in Staten Island lore. Stories like fighting off 7 guys at once while in a bar, their escapades were wild enough that romanticized them even more.

Staten Island was the wilderness compared to Brooklyn. It was full of trees, fields, and quiet streets that seemed to stretch endlessly. We'd spend hours running around the fields, catching frogs, our sneakers muddy and our shirts sticking to our backs from the heat. We'd laugh all day as we chased one another, racing through the tall grass. Anthony and Vincent would hammer together treehouses from whatever wood they could "borrow" from nearby construction sites. We'd sit up there like we were kings of our little patch of the island, sharing stories and planning adventures.

As the streetlights flickered on, we'd hop on our bikes and head back, just in time for a dinner of pasta, meatballs, and sausage. Afterward, the whole family would gather around the dining room table, playing poker for hours. It was our ritual, a warm, familiar pulse that filled the room with shouting matches, laughter, and the clinking of coins late into the night.

One weekend, my cousin Anthony, who was around ten at the time and full of piss-and-vinegar, decided to challenge my dad to a bicycle race. Now, my dad was a joker, always teasing his nephews, so he shot back, "Oh yeah? I'll not only race you, but I'll have Richie riding on the handlebars!" This sounded like the best idea in the world to me and Anthony, so we lined up, the summer sun blazing down on us, practically daring us to go faster. I could feel the adrenaline coursing through me as we took off, pushing forward like we were racing the Tour de Staten Island.

We were neck and neck with Anthony only a few yards into the race when we hit a pothole the size of a sewer cap. The bike stopped short, but we didn't. I went flying over the handlebars, skidding across the hot pavement, with my dad crashing down right on top of me. The race turned into a shock of pain as I hit the ground. In that instant, all the laughter and cheers faded, replaced by the reality of the accident and the aftermath that would follow.

I felt a pain in my jaw so sharp it was killing me, and I couldn't stop crying. There I was, lying on the street, dust and sweat sticking to my cheeks, tears streaming down, and I just wailed. For hours, I blamed my dad for that crash, but how could I blame him? He only wanted to be a cool dad and have fun with us. He must have felt terrible, but I didn't let up. Even after he took me to the Italian festival on Richmond Avenue to cheer me up, I was still bawling. The pain in my jaw made it impossible to speak or even chew any food, turning what should have been a fun outing into a torture session. For two weeks, it was nothing but tears and moaning. Every attempt my parents made to comfort me only seemed to make it worse.

Finally, after seeing me barely talking or eating, my parents took me to the dentist who looked at my jaw and told them it was broken. "Too late to fix now," he said, shaking his head. "It's already started to heal on its own."

Just like that, I was stuck with a fuckin' crooked jaw. To top it off, I had to eat baby food for three months. Three long months in first grade, sitting at the lunch table with mush while the other kids called me names.

Isn't grammar school hard enough? I should've just had my parents set up a highchair at school; it wouldn't have made a difference with all the teasing I got. I learned to cope by turning the teasing into a joke, making light of it with some good old self-deprecating humor. It didn't stop the comments, but at least I could feel like I was in on the joke, turning the whole thing into something I could laugh about, even if it stung a little inside.

It was so much fun at my aunt's house until the fighting began. Anthony and Vincent were a couple of crazy bastards. They'd brawl as part of their daily routine, fistfights that would sometimes spill right out onto the street. The neighbors didn't even look twice; it was just another day on the block. My uncle, a big, broad-shouldered guy who'd shave every morning and still have a 5 o'clock shadow by noon, would storm outside, grabbing the two of them by whatever body part he could get a hold of and yanking them in the house. Once they were in, he laid into them himself, kicking and punching them up the stairs and back down, determined to knock some sense into them. I'd run and hide in the closet of my cousin's bedroom until the yelling and pounding stopped. The whole house would feel tense, like the walls themselves were bracing for the next round.

My parents acted like what happened to my cousins was just another family secret, turning a blind eye to tension so thick you could choke on it. But I felt every blow, like I was the one getting hit. When things got too heated or that heavy silence filled their house—just like when my parents wouldn't speak in ours—I'd slip away, lock myself in a room, heart pounding. I'd whisper to God, hoping my connection with Him could calm the storm and bring us peace.

Birthday parties weren't much better for me. My cousin Mario, who was a lot older and meaner, would show up, and when no one was paying attention, he'd drag me into a bedroom and lock the door. Once inside, he'd throw me against the walls. Then he'd punch the shit out of me in places where the bruises wouldn't show. The finale: he'd pull my pants down, lay my peesh on the dresser, and slam it with his fist. I remember feeling completely helpless, unable to escape or scream for help. Then he'd stare me down, that smirk on his face, and tell me that if I told anyone, it'd be worse next time.

So, like with a lot of things in life, I kept quiet. I'd sit through those birthday parties with my cousins, trying to enjoy them, while that big jerk was just waiting to ruin it for me. Before Mario even walked through the door, I was already bracing myself for what was coming. I knew exactly how things would play out, like some exhausting routine I couldn't escape. Birthday parties should've been fun, but for me, they felt like something to survive. I'd catch myself watching the clock, waiting for it all to be over, hoping I'd make it through without the usual shit. I felt trapped in a cycle of fear and shame, missing out on the fun while pretending everything was normal around the others. The stress weighed on me long before the first person even arrived... it just sucked.

When I slept over at my cousin Anthony's on the weekends, things were a little calmer, but he had his own ways of stirring up trouble. We'd be up at the crack of dawn, ready to deliver newspapers to every house in the neighborhood. Anthony had a stolen supermarket wagon piled high with papers, and we'd push it down the street. But as we went along, he eyed anything left out on a lawn—bikes, balls, even old sports gear.

With this naughty grin, he'd turn to me and say, "Hey, look at that! These kids are gettin' rid of this stuff for free. Let's take it!" And just like that, our wagon would get heavier, loaded with our "new" toys. When we got back to his house, he'd spray-paint the bikes a different color, covering up any evidence that they didn't actually belong to us.

As he got older, he graduated to cars, painting them just as quickly and quietly as he had with the bikes. Before long, both Anthony and Vincent started showing up in fancy cars, wearing tracksuits, with pockets full of cash—and no one ever asked where it all came from.

Looking back, the signs were all there, clear as a fall day over Staten Island. But to me back then, it was all just a part of life with family, the adventures of growing up together intertwined with a lot of turmoil.

Chapter 5

The Boy Scouts of Bensonhurst

I had to duck and dodge rocks flying over the cemetery fence from other kids on the four-block walk to my Boy Scout meetings, wearing my uniform like a badge of honor. But in Bensonhurst, being a Boy Scout wasn't exactly cool. Knot-tying and camping? Nah, they didn't get it. They were all about stickball in the street, dreaming of being Tom Seaver. That was their thing. But I wasn't your regular scout, nor was our troop.

Driving through Times Square in a van packed with my friends was one of my first wild ventures as a scout. We had just come from a wrestling match at Madison Square Garden, and our scoutmaster, Nick DiMarco, decided to show us what he called "the real New York City."

Knowing Mr. DiMarco, it was bound to be an experience. He took us straight into the heart of Times

Square, back when it wasn't the family-friendly tourist trap it is today. Instead, it was a chaotic circus filled with hookers, drunks, and squeegee guys crowding every red light.

Sitting in that van, we were a bunch of 11- and 12-year-olds with front-row seats to the freak show. The characters outside seemed to love the fact that we were just kids, wide-eyed and out of place. At one point, a hooker leaned right into Mr. DiMarco's open window. She fiddled with the radio, cranking up some Donna Summer, and then went for his pants like it was just another part of her routine. She yelled, "Turn up those tunes!" while grabbing his peesh, leaving us hysterically laughing, but also in a bit of panic.

Mr. DiMarco hit the gas, trying to get us out of there, but it was already too late. By the time we sped off, she'd swiped his wallet clean. Now we were stuck—no money for tolls to get back to Brooklyn, sitting in a van full of broke Boy Scouts. He told us to get out of the van and panhandle for just enough cash to pay the tolls.

Imagine the sight of us, asking strangers for a few bucks just to make it home. Can you imagine trying to explain this to our mothers? "Yeah, Ma, we went to a wrestling match, saw some hookers, and begged for toll money. How was your night?"

When we weren't busy dodging prostitutes and squeegee guys, we were out camping in places like Staten Island or New Jersey. Now, camping with our troop wasn't exactly like what most Boy Scouts did. Sure, there were structured activities and lessons, but we had our own idea of fun. Instead of swimming lessons at the lake, we'd sneak onto the roof of our cabin, lay out towels, and get a golden tan. It was like our own private tanning salon—one story up, out of sight, and completely against the rules. If the scout leaders came looking for us, all they had to do was look up. But let's be honest, why would they think about checking the roof?

When we actually did take part in camp events, we didn't just show up—we owned them. Take the annual Klondike Derby, for example. The challenge was to build a snow sled and race it, and of course, we couldn't settle for something basic. We decided to "Brooklyn-ize" our sled by adding hood ornaments from cars. So, we went hunting for them in the middle of the night, sneaking out of the camp to roam the streets of Staten Island. Tween boys creeping around in the dark, prying hood ornaments off cars that looked like they were "falling off anyway." It wasn't exactly what you'd picture when you think of Boy Scouts.

The sled race itself was another story. Whether or not there was snow on the ground, the race went on. Pulling a sled loaded with a 140-pound kid over rocky terrain without snow was brutal. Back then, nobody thought twice about it. You just did it, and if you scraped your knees or pulled a muscle, you sucked it up. Try that today, and parents would be calling lawyers, saying their kids were scarred for life.

Camping gave us a ton of stories I just can't forget. This is one of those stories that'll get "caught up" in your mind for sure.

It was a freezing morning, and instead of the usual 7 a.m. bugle call, the whole camp woke up to the high-pitched scream of an 11-year-old scout. Now, at camp, a scream like that only means one of two things: something awful involving an assistant scoutmaster or a zipper disaster. Luckily, or unluckily, it was the latter. The kid's hands must've been too numb from the cold to feel what he was doing, but his little guy wasn't so lucky. When he zipped up his pants, the zipper caught his peesh, and, well, it was a bloody mess.

Me and Rob heard the screams and started running toward them. But then the screaming suddenly stopped, like when a baby cries so hard, they can't catch their breath. Scouts were darting around, yelling, "Some kid's wiener is stuck in his zipper!"

When we got there, we saw the poor kid. Sure enough, the zipper's teeth had clamped down hard on his little pecker. The look on his face—and on the faces of everyone standing around—said it all. Not a single one of us wanted to go near him. I mean, who's volunteering to yank a kid's peesh out of a zipper? Not me, that's for sure.

So, me and Rob, being the cowards we were, backed off and headed toward breakfast instead. As we stood in line waiting for our scrambled eggs and sausage links, we heard the sweet sound of an ambulance pulling into camp. At least the kid was finally going to get some real help. But after seeing what we saw, eating those sausage links wasn't easy. Every bite made us think of the poor kid's situation.

Those memories come rushing back to me often, reminding me how much those experiences shaped who I am today. Camp taught me to communicate with people, build the courage to face a crowd, and handle emergencies. And nothing sums it up better than the time I had my infamous run-in with an ax.

It all started with an ax-chopping contest, something every scout looked forward to. There were about ten contestants, each trying to prove we had what it took to chop a log the fastest. The others were swinging shiny, two-handed axes. Me? I was using an old, beat-up hatchet that looked like it should've been retired years ago. But I wasn't going to let that stop me.

The judge blew the whistle to start, his cheeks puffed out like Dizzy Gillespie playing the trumpet. The crowd of about three hundred circled around us, screaming and cheering for their favorites. The energy was electric, and my adrenaline was pumping. I started hacking away at the log like a woodpecker on a mission. Chips of wood were flying everywhere, and the crowd kept edging closer and closer with excitement.

Then it happened. One second, I was chopping like a madman, and the next, the head of my hatchet fucking flew off the handle. It shot 20 feet into the air, spinning like a top. For a second, everything went silent. I couldn't hear the crowd anymore and everything seemed to move in slow motion.

And then, the hatchet head came down, slicing right through my hand. It missed my skull by inches, but I'll never forget the sight when I looked down. The bone between my finger pointer and thumb was completely exposed, and blood was spurting out with every beat of my heart.

The shock hit me, and my mind was racing with confusion and the sinking feeling that I'd just lost the contest. But before I could even think about what to do, a swarm of scouts and leaders surrounded me. Every one of them wanted to show off their First Aid Merit Badge skills. Within minutes, I was bandaged up like a mummy and on my way to the hospital.

Eighteen stitches later, I was patched up and lucky that the nerve damage was minimal. When I called my mom from the hospital, she asked if I wanted to be picked up. I told her I wanted to stay because I didn't want to let my troop down by leaving early. She was proud of me for sticking it out, but if I'm honest, the real reason I stayed was for something a little less noble. Jimmy had gotten his hands on a few of his older brother's Playboy magazines, and I wasn't about to miss that.

When I got back to camp, I was treated like a hero. Scouts crowded around to hear the story, but for me, the best reward wasn't the glory, it was Miss March. Ahhhh, summer camp... nothing else like it.

As you might expect, after my "hero's welcome" and our victorious gawking at Jimmy's stash of *Playboy* magazines, we were full of pent-up energy. Let's face it, being a group of rowdy teenage boys in the woods, there wasn't much to do with all that frustration but channel it into mischief. Naturally, our attention turned to Troop 484.

We hated them with every fiber of our adolescent beings. They were the goody-two-shoes of the camp—

the ones who always had spotless uniforms, perfect formations, and badges for everything. It was nauseating. So, we plotted with flashlights in hand and revenge in our hearts and set off under the cover of night to their pristine little campsite.

Once there, we moved like shadows, creeping to their firepit to start a fire. We stacked log after log onto the small flames until the fire roared into a proper bonfire. The flames lit up their tents, casting shadows and setting the stage for what came next. We circled their tents like Crazy Horse's warriors surrounding General Custer at Little Bighorn. If memory serves correct, Custer didn't stand a chance, and neither did the boys of Troop 484.

When I gave the signal, we pounced. We leaped onto their tents like maniacs, collapsing them right on top of the poor kids inside. Through the nylon tents, we delivered body blows as the unsuspecting scouts screamed in fear and a little pain. Their high-pitched shrieks fueled our frenzy, but we didn't stick around long. Within minutes, we were gone, leaving behind a raging fire and a campsite full of shaken scouts.

You'd think that'd be enough for one night, right? Nope. We weren't done. There was one more score to settle. You see, there was this bossy kid in our own troop. This kid thought he ran the place, but we had other plans for him. Armed with rope and a desire for payback, me, Rob, Michael, and Paul went hunting for him.

We found him fast asleep on a cot in the cabin. Quietly, we each grabbed a side of the cot, lifted it off the ground, and carried him outside without waking him. Once we had him under a big tree, we lashed the cot with rope and tossed the ends over a thick branch about 15 feet up. Slowly and carefully, we hoisted him into the air. When he was dangling high enough to make our point, we tied off the ropes and headed back to the cabin.

It wasn't until about 4 a.m. that we heard him crying like a baby, waking up to find himself suspended in the air. Looking back now, what if he woke and just fell to the ground? Geez... you don't think of the consequences of your actions as a kid, I guess.

A couple of months after I got hit by that car while waiting at the bus stop, I felt good enough to finally attend a scout meeting. It was my first time back, and a lot had happened since my last meeting. For one, they hired a new assistant scoutmaster.

The minute I met him, my Spidey-Sense went off. There was something about the way he stared at me as he shook my hand. It just didn't feel right to me. Turns out, my instincts were dead on. He pulled me aside during the meeting, acting all friendly and concerned, and asked how my leg was doing after the accident. At first, I thought he was just being nice, but then the conversation took a turn. He told me he used to be an EMT and said he couldn't believe my leg hadn't broken when I got hit. I was trying to be polite and respectful, answering his questions, but then he crossed the line. He asked me to come down to the basement so he could "take a look" at my leg in private.

I knew enough back then to realize it wasn't a good situation. My gut told me to get out of there. I told him no, said I was fine, and that I'd already been checked out by plenty of doctors. Then I pushed past him and went to the kitchen to grab some water, hoping that it'd be the end of it. But it wasn't. He followed me. I could feel him standing right behind me, and then he leaned in and whispered, *"Come on."*

I bolted out of the building, and before I could explain the situation to the scoutmaster, the bogus molester came running out to spin his version of the story. It took a few days of digging before they uncovered the truth about him. Turns out, he'd been hopping from troop to troop, either molesting kids or trying to. Back then, there weren't background checks or systems in place to catch predators like him. He preyed on boys he thought were vulnerable. And for whatever reason, he thought he'd found an easy target in me.

But somehow, I saw through him. I trusted my gut and got myself out of that situation. It makes me wonder, though... how did I have the smarts as a kid to see through someone like him, but as an adult, I couldn't see through the idiots in other forms?

Anyway, after years of loafing around and procrastinating, I finally managed to stop procrastinating and work toward Eagle Scout, which is the highest rank in the Boy Scouts. I had two tasks left to get it, and time wasn't on my side—only a few months until I turned 18, which meant I would not be eligible any longer.

The first thing on my list was the Eagle project. This was no walk in the park. You had to demonstrate a whole bunch of skills like planning, leadership, budgeting, and believe it or not, compassion. I sat there, racking my brain, thinking, "Richie, think! What can I do to knock this out of the park?" Then it hit me. I came up with an idea that would kill two birds with one stone: I could knock out my Eagle project *and* satisfy my other desire—being around girls. Yeah, you heard me right.

So, I went back to my roots... to Fontbonne's theater director and asked if I could act, direct, and handle the marketing for their next musical. I threw in a little extra twist: I suggested we add a performance that would benefit a local orphanage and even invite the kids from the orphanage to attend. She loved the idea. What I didn't tell her was that this was all part of my Eagle Scout requirements. Why should I? It was a good cause, right?

Let's be real for a second. I couldn't let the girls at the school find out that I was involved with the Boy Scouts. My reputation with them was already on shaky ground. I didn't need more gossip about my masculinity floating around. So, I had to come up with a game plan to keep the two worlds separate, while somehow still making them work together. Sounds complicated, right? But trust me, I had it figured out.

I kept the scout leaders completely in the dark about the musical practices and everything else involving the school. When I wrote the press release about the orphanage performance, I kept it vague, just saying it was a "nice thing" I was doing for the community. The leaders didn't know the full story, and the girls didn't either. They just thought I was a good guy doing a good thing for the less fortunate. It worked like a charm.

The whole thing went off without a hitch. The girls saw me as a stud, and the scouts, well, they just thought I was doing a solid community service project. Win-

win. But I wasn't out of the woods yet. I also made sure the scouts sat at the back of the theater, so the orphanage kids could sit up front. It was a ton of work and more stress than I care to admit, but in the end, it turned out to be a huge success. But even with that behind me, I still had one more thing to tackle.

The last thing I had left to finish was the Citizenship in the World merit badge. I'd been working on it for months, but this was the hardest merit badge I'd ever come across. Now, I was just a week away from turning 18, and I knew if I didn't get this signed off by an instructor before my birthday, I'd miss out on the chance to earn my Eagle Scout. Talk about pressure!

So, I reached out to Mr. Grillo, the local instructor who was qualified to review my work, test me on it, and ultimately sign off that I had completed the assignments. I gave him a call and he was excited for me, but that excitement dropped the second I told him I only had a few days left to finish.

He was like, "Richie, I work all week, and my daughter's wedding is this Saturday. There's no way I can do all that testing and reviewing in time." There was silence for a second, and then he surprised me. He said, "Look, come to my house before the wedding on Saturday morning, and I'll test you then."

I couldn't believe it. That was very generous of him. This is what scouting is supposed to be about.

So, there I was, up early on a Saturday morning, heading to Mr. Grillo's house at 8:30 a.m. I knocked on the door, and the wedding photographer answered. He told me that Mr. Grillo was expecting me and to head upstairs to his bedroom. I walked up, knocked on the door, and Mr. Grillo shouted for me to come in. Now, this is where it gets interesting.

There he was, running around his room in his boxers and garters holding up the socks. His tuxedo shirt was on, but no bow tie yet because he was having a hard time with it. He tossed it to me and asked if I knew how to tie one. I gave it a shot. Lucky for him, I knew my knots and how to tie a tie.

While he was ironing his pants, he started firing off questions at me about the merit badge stuff, and I answered them to his satisfaction. When we were done, he grabbed my certificate, signed it, and told me he was proud to have signed off on my last requirement for Eagle Scout.

We went downstairs together and there was his daughter in her dress. I got to see her for the first time at the same moment as her dad did. It was nice to witness all that happiness on such a special day.

Years later, I ran into Mr. Grillo at a restaurant in Manhattan. He was there with his wife, daughter, son-in-law, and new grandson. I went up to their table to say hello, and as soon as he saw me, he shouted "RICHIE!" so loud that the whole dining room turned their heads. He practically leaped over the table to give me a hug.

I told him I'd never forget what he did for me that Saturday morning, and his daughter laughed and said they'd never forget me either. We shared a good laugh about that. There were some great people in scouting who really made their mark on my life, and Mr. Grillo was definitely one of them.

Chapter 6

Teenage Tomfoolery

I imagine most people's lives are shaped by their teenage years. For me, those years at Xaverian High in Bay Ridge, Brooklyn, were a time of discovering who I was and what I was capable of. High school was a mix of experiences that truly shaped my personality and outlook on life. I learned to think on my feet, to sometimes take a leap of faith, and to face crises head-on. While I didn't always feel fearless, each challenge taught me something new about resilience and stepping up when it counted.

Xaverian, an elite private school that faced the Narrows, was fucking crazy hard for me in its own way, but the real adventure often started with the bus rides there and back. Every day, I hopped on the B4 bus at my stop on 16th Avenue and 75th Street, right in the heart of Brooklyn. The bus ride itself became a tradition, a part of my routine that was anything but mundane.

We loved cramming into the back seats, our own little world. We would joke, tease, and laugh at the front-seat kids. Those rides weren't just trips because sometimes they were the best part of our day. Oh geez, the shit we got into drove the bus driver nuts! We'd pop open the sunroof like we owned the bus, daring each other to stick our heads through during the ride. Then there was the classic move of spitting on the ceiling, taking bets on which one would hang on the longest before gravity took its toll and fell on an unsuspecting passenger.

On those rides, we'd roast each other like marshmallows over an open fire. It was all good fun, until it wasn't, and we'd take it a little too far. You know how it is. Insults would fly, laughter would erupt, and before you knew it, someone would be throwing a punch. But the next day, we were friends again! So yeah, those B4 bus rides to school were something else.

But my second week at the bus stop could have changed my life forever. A brown Cadillac slowly passed by. I noticed the driver looking over at me, but I didn't pay much attention because I was already thinking about what I was going to do after school. The car came around again, but this time he pulled over at the bus stop. He rolled down the window and asked me what school I was headed to. So, I told him I was on my way to Xaverian.

He pointed to his back seat and said, "That's great, get in. I'm taking these two girls down that way too." I took a gander at the two girls in the back seat. They seemed older than me, hotter than the usual girls on the bus. They looked at me, and that was all I needed! They opened the back door and told me to sit between them. I thanked them up and down because I thought I might have missed my regular bus.

I can still see the driver's devilish smile in the rearview mirror as one of the girls leaned over and said, "I love the way your balls look in those jeans." I didn't know if the blood was rushing to my face or somewhere else. All of a sudden, I had both girls' hands all over me. You'd think this is every freshman boy's fantasy—and it was just for a fleeting moment. But then, I felt something was definitely wrong with this picture. Girls fondling me wasn't a usual bus ride to school.

So, I told him to pull over, pretending I'd forgotten my Algebra textbook at home. He wasn't having it, but I saw a red light coming up. I reached over the brunette, who smelled amazing (maybe I should've stayed), opened the door, crawled over her, and jumped out of the car. The sleazebag slowly followed me down the block and told me to get back in, and so did the girls.

But I walked back in the opposite direction so they couldn't follow me.

I chickened out of what every boy or man desires, but it was probably the best decision I made as a kid. Who knows what could've happened—maybe I'd have been abducted, hurt, or wound up dead under the bridge like Father George!

Just when I thought my second week of high school couldn't end soon enough, my first altercation with a high school bully came into play. Xaverian was an all-boys college preparatory school. Yes... I went to an all-boys Catholic school. My first period was biology at the end of the north wing.

As I'm walking with all my books, I see a commotion down the hall, near my classroom. As I get closer, I see a bunch of seniors sitting on the floor against the lockers, with one kid who had a broken leg. The biggest guy was using that kid's crutch to block anyone trying to pass in the hall. If you said you were a freshman, he told you to turn around and go the other way.

When I finally reached the stretched-out crutch, he asked if I was a freshman, and I answered yes. He prodded me with the end of the crutch and told me to go all the way around the school just to get to the classroom that was only feet away.

I'm not sure what came over me, but I threw my stack of textbooks at him and snatched the crutch from his hands. I began pounding him with the crutch as all the other kids started cheering me on. He cowered in the corner like a wimp as the gym teacher, Mr. Hickey, ran over to save him.

The teacher grabbed my arm and took me into an empty classroom. He said that I couldn't do that to a senior, especially since he was the captain of the wrestling team. He said I should channel that anger and join the team too. I told him I would think about it, even though I had no interest in rubbing my body against other sweaty guys.

I went back to the hall, gathered all my books, and the wrestler came over to me and said I better watch myself because nobody makes a fool of him.

My relationship with my cousin Anthony was like having a secret weapon. After school that day, I called him to tell him about the incident with the bully, knowing he was the kind of guy who would have my back no matter what.

The next day, Anthony showed up at school with some random girl and his friend Mongo. I met them at the bus stop, pointed out the kid who had caused trouble, and within minutes, Mongo had the bully by the neck, telling him never to mess with me again. That moment made me feel invincible, knowing Anthony and Mongo had my back. From then on, my high school years were worry-free—nobody bothered me.

Xaverian High was a huge adjustment for me. Coming from Our Lady of Guadalupe where the workload was much more laid-back, stepping into Xaverian felt like a culture shock. At Our Lady of Guadalupe, I could coast through my work with ease, but at Xaverian, it was really difficult work. The pressure was on, and I quickly realized that my usual laid-back approach wasn't going to cut it anymore. This school was intense, and I had to step up my game in ways I never had to before.

In my first year, they had what was called saturation courses. Most of the course load was given in the language you chose to study. Mine was Italian so naturally I wasn't doing well in the other classes. Talk about masochists! I was failing, so it was time to see Mr. Alto, the guidance counselor, for—I guess—a little guidance.

He asked me a series of questions about why I thought I wasn't doing well. He asked how I studied, where I studied, if I studied with the door closed, and—the question that rubbed me (ha) the wrong way—"Do you masturbate while you're studying?"

Now that's a tricky question. How can I do that if I'm studying? Maybe if he phrased the question differently, I could've answered him the way this creep wanted so he could get his jollies.

At first, I tried to coast through classes, relying on charm over effort. But I soon realized my disengagement was holding me back and needed to step up and put in the work. It wasn't enough that I was struggling in school and fighting with seniors, but then I had to get mugged on the way home too.

It was a miserable, rainy day when I was walking with my friends, Pete and Mark, on our way to the bus stop. From under my umbrella, I noticed two guys across the street watching us, but I didn't think much of it. All of a sudden, they came from behind us, grabbed me and Pete, and held friggin' knives to our throats. They ripped Pete's gold chain off his neck and took whatever money we had in our pockets. Mark, meanwhile, was standing there, more concerned about missing the bus. To add salt to the wound, the bastards came right back and snatched our umbrellas, leaving us soaked waiting for the bus.

It felt like we had no defense against them while they had knives, and I just kept thinking how badly I wanted to cross paths with them again someday. We didn't report it to the school or the cops. Where we grew up, you didn't do that. You didn't rely on the cops; you handled it your own way, through our own method.

A few days later, justice came to my school. During my free class, I was sitting on the windowsill, staring out into the parking lot, wondering why I was stuck at an all-boys school. That's when I spotted one of the guys who mugged us. He was trying to cut the lock off a bike. My blood boiled.

I ran to the lunchroom and grabbed a few friends to help me confront him. When my friends and I got outside, he spotted us and took off running. We chased him for three blocks, where he bolted into a candy store, and when we followed him inside, the owner kicked us out, saying no fighting in his place.

It turned out that kid hung out there often, so Pete told his older brother who was a guy with a reputation for being nuts. A week later, Pete came to school with a huge grin and his gold necklace around his neck. His brother had tracked the guy down and got it back from him, though we never learned the details of how it went down. That whole experience didn't change my feelings about justice—it only cemented them. It wasn't about feeling safe anymore; it was about knowing that you had to take matters into your own hands when the system didn't work for you.

While going to school, I got my first job working at Burger King on 86th Street. There were a lot of cool kids working there, and I started coming into my own in terms of my speaking skills, but my Whopper-making skills left a little to be desired. I was very slow making them because I made sure the pickles looked perfect, the ketchup was squirted on like a pinwheel, and the lettuce wasn't coming out of the sides of the bun.

As I was developing my masterpieces, the customers lined up, waiting for their "fast food." The manager grabbed me and let me know he was bumping me down to regular burgers and fries. Nothing really changed... the lines of frustrated customers didn't get any better. The following week, I was told I would be relegated to the dining room, cleaning tables, and the bathrooms. I wasn't crazy about it because fishing Kotex and tampons out of the ladies' room toilet wasn't my calling.

On my way to work one afternoon, I was on the bus with this girl, Theresa, who I liked from an all-girls school, Fontbonne Hall Academy. I was in love with a different girl from this school on a weekly basis. If they just looked at me and twirled their hair, I was infatuated and imagined walking down the aisle in a tux.

Anyway, we had to transfer from one bus to another to get where we both had to go. As we approached the traffic light, I saw our next bus across the avenue waiting at the light. I knew if we missed that bus, we'd be stuck for at least another half hour or longer! So, I decided to take a chance and show how chivalry wasn't dead as a horny teenager.

I took off like a shot and ran from the bus to catch the connecting one. This is where I get hit by a car again! My mind was so engrossed in Theresa that I ran into oncoming traffic. The next thing I saw was the front grill of a Plymouth Grand Fury, and I was an easy-moving target. BOOM! The trees in the park start flipping upside down and back again a couple of times. Oh, wait! That's me flipping around like a ragdoll.

I wound up about thirty feet from the spot where I was hit and came to a stop in front of our connecting bus. As Theresa was screaming and I was lying there, I thought to myself, I could get a sympathy date with her, but the numbness disappeared, and the pain kicked in. The ambulance came, brought me to the hospital, and I didn't even break a bone. How's that possible? I never did get that sympathy date with Theresa because she started dating someone else while I was recovering. I'd like to think that the near-death experience was the reason we didn't date and not the fact that she wasn't into me. I mean, how do you not go out with me after I provide you with an amazing circus act?

The girls of Fontbonne did a number on me. I even infiltrated their school by joining their drama club. They needed boys to play the male roles, and it was right up my alley. I had a free pass into the school. Picture one boy strutting like Patrick Swayze around an all-girls school.

I was in paradise until I started dating Rosemarie LaRusso. She was a perfect girl for me to date because she knew everyone, and she would be able to catapult me into meeting other girls. The problem with Rosemarie was that she was light years ahead of me. She would tell me about all her past boyfriends, the guys she saw at summer camp, and the boys that are away at college who she couldn't wait to see when they came home.

Talk about a turn-off. So, for those reasons, I never even kissed her. The "relationship" lasted about a month, but the repercussions lasted a long time at Fontbonne. Rosemarie couldn't figure out why I didn't kiss her. Me being such a great communicator, I didn't tell her that after our talks, I might as well have been castrated. It couldn't be anything she said or did because she was Miss Perfect, so she spread a rumor at her school that I was gay.

Being portrayed as gay in the '80s wasn't exactly what it is today. The rumor spread like a pandemic. I would ask girls out and kept getting rejected. I didn't find out until I was in for a while that I had the gay label. Geez... I should've dumped that girl after her first boyfriend-in-the-back-of-his-van story, and I would've been the Casanova of Fontbonne—well, not Casanova, but I might have gotten a couple of dates here and there.

On the last day of junior year, my friend Pete and I have the last two periods free, which means we get to go home at about noon. Who's better than us? What could ruin this day? Someone pulling the fire alarm at 9 a.m.?

Brother Franklin, our principal, got on the loudspeaker and told us we all have detention at the end of the day. Juniors and seniors report to the gym, and freshmen and sophomores report to the auditorium. Attendance will be taken, and whoever doesn't attend will be expelled from the school.

Pete and I are in a quandary. We can stay for the two periods until 2:45 p.m. or take a chance and leave at noon, hoping he doesn't take attendance. Naturally, we chose the latter, and guess what? He did take attendance, and the only two assholes who didn't stay were Pete and me. Again, Brother Franklin got on the loudspeaker and announced Pete and I were going to be expelled and sorry that all the students didn't get a chance to say goodbye to us. That sarcastic bastard.

I was lucky that my sister was home that afternoon, and I begged her to answer the phone by posing as my mother. She did me the favor, and sure enough, I had to report to school the next morning at 8 a.m. Pete and I were shitting a pill.

We met Brother Franklin in his office, and he was PISSED—or, in his words, IRKED. What the fuck does "irked" mean? It sounded pretty bad, and as a student at a preparatory school, I guess I should've known. Well, the "irked" principal had our school files on his desk, ready to de-pants us about our past history at the school. He took an old, failed test that I crumpled up two years ago. It looked like they ironed out all the wrinkles and added it to my file just for an event like this.

He's like, "This test paper represents the failure you are at Xaverian." Wow, just stab me in the gut and twist the knife, why don't ya?

He berated us for a while and threatened expulsion, but in the end, he gave us two weeks of summer school detention—full days! I dressed for the beach those two weeks so my mother wouldn't suspect anything and had my clothes in a gym bag. The things you gotta do to

keep your parents out of your business in high school...
geez!

Looking back at my time at Xaverian High, I realize I wasn't the same person at the end of high school as I was when I started. Deep down, I struggled with confidence, and that insecurity shaped how I presented myself to everyone. I became a bully and a showman, putting on a façade that masked my true feelings. It took me years to find myself.

The atmosphere at Xaverian was a mix of discipline and intelligence. For me, it was so challenging. I didn't take full advantage of the tools and resources Xaverian offered. I would go to class, but I was only half engaged, more focused on getting through the day than truly absorbing what was being taught. There was so much potential around me, but I was skimming the surface, missing out on the opportunities to dive in and really make the most of my time there.

Chapter 7

Fists and Friendships

I started hanging out with a new crew that lived in the Bath Beach section of Brooklyn. It was a part of Bensonhurst, full of Wise Guys and Wanna-Be's. I met Jimmy and Rob at Boy Scouts when we were around nine years old. After a while, we started hanging out on the corner of Bay 13th and Benson Avenue. We spent our time playing football, softball, and paddleball or just shooting the breeze. Those moments really brought us together and created friendships that have lasted a lifetime. It was a quiet area that was also taken over by Italians. We played ball all day and didn't stop until night. We were a solid group, surrounded by some pretty bad people.

The friendships from Bay 13th have been lifelong bonds that shaped who I am. Through all the ups and downs, their loyalty and support have been my strength. I'm grateful to have them, reminding me of the power of loyalty and shared history. With those bonds, we had some outrageous moments—and Halloweens in Brooklyn were some of those times.

Halloween was insane back then. You had to deal with egg-throwing, mischief night antics, and people scaring the piss out of you. I was never one who enjoyed the day. I'd stay on edge, constantly watching out, always expecting an egg to fly my way. I hated the day, especially after we had to kick the crap out of a Made Guy's son.

We were sitting on my Paulie's stoop when these kids started throwing rocks at us instead of eggs. I guess these kids improvised and grabbed rocks to substitute for eggs. One of the rocks hit me in the hand, and I was fuckin' pissed, so we took off after them. Rob and I were fast. We caught up to the kid and beat the hell out of him. What we didn't realize was that his father was a captain in the Bonanno Crime Family.

We laughed for hours until black Cadillacs started showing up like sharks circling a school of baby seals. It seemed the kid was pretty banged up, but thank God, he wasn't hospitalized. I almost crapped my pants and couldn't believe who this kid was related to.

Rob and I ran to his girlfriend's house to hide out. He suggested I punch him in the face with a rock to make it look like he'd gotten hurt by one. At first, it sounded like a good idea, but I wasn't about to punch my best friend in the face. He tried it himself, but it wasn't hard enough, so his girlfriend picked up a rock and—WHAM!—she nailed him right in the cheek.

We laughed hysterically, but we knew we'd have to face the music sooner or later. Jimmy called to tell us we were screwed because his brother, who was also connected, got a call to rat us out. So, we went to Rob's father, who was somehow connected too. Are you getting the point that everyone was connected somehow back then?

Rob's dad went to the Bonanno club on Bath Avenue and told them who he was. We had to have a sit-down in the club to work it all out. We waited a couple of days and it felt like forever.

Finally, when we arrived at the meeting, there was the kid, looking a little mangled, sitting with his goombah father. We sat down at a poker table in the back room of the social club. It reeked of smoke, alcohol, and the lingering presence of a couple of chopped-up bodies. Everyone in the place smoked like chimneys and tossed back drinks served by a girl from a makeshift bar. It looked like they never put a dime into the space. The wood-paneled walls gave it that old, almost claustrophobic feel. I sensed that a lot of guys who crossed the Bonannos came into this place but didn't leave the same way.

The kid's father said he'd heard his son's version of things and now he wanted to hear ours. I immediately launched into my version—no pauses, no hesitation. The second I mentioned the word "rock," the guy turned to his son with a look of disgust. I finished telling the story, but at that point, he didn't need to hear the rest. He said he'd heard we were good kids, that his son had a lot to learn from us, and that he deserved a beating.

How do you like those apples? I began to breathe again. You never knew who was connected to who back then. That shit could've helped me on the paddle ball courts playing against Steve Ferragamo.

Steve Ferragamo was a well-known neighborhood mobster. He had done 21 years in prison but was released through the Innocence Project after being convicted of the brutal rape of a police officer's wife while her husband was tied up and forced to watch. Whether he actually did it or not, Ferragamo had a reputation for being a hothead. I admired him because everyone feared him. He wasn't just good at being a gangster, he was also a phenomenal paddleball player. He was a fixture at the Dyker Park courts.

One day, I was playing a match on the court behind him, and after a while, he started watching us. I was pretty good myself, but Ferragamo didn't know me from Adam (who *is* Adam, anyway?).

He asked me to play a game with him. So, we started playing, and I was super focused, playing like Rafael Nadal—except better-looking, at least in my mind. I wanted to win so badly, but I was worried if I won because of his legendary temper. I was in a no-win situation. The more points I scored, the bigger the audience grew, and the more pissed Ferragamo became. Then he finally lost it.

The ball went outside the fence after I smashed a killer shot off the bottom of the wall. Ferragamo snapped and yelled, "Go get the ball, big nose."

I saw red, and at that moment, the game didn't matter. I went nose to nose (pun intended) with him and told him to go fuck himself.

You could see his whole demeanor shift in an instant. He took his paddle, patted me on the head, and said to everyone watching that I was a "brave little bastard." That was the last time we played paddleball, but it wasn't the last time we almost came to blows.

After that paddleball incident, things settled down for a long while. But if you know anything about growing up in Brooklyn, it's like trouble's always just around the corner. No matter what, it finds you. The thing with Ferragamo wasn't the end of the line; it was the first of another chaotic moment.

One sunny day, Jimmy and I were hanging out on the corner of Bay 13th, just enjoying the weather. Jimmy was always the kid with the "resting smirk face." No matter what he was thinking, people always assumed he was laughing at them, which always got him in trouble—and today was no exception. As we were waiting for our crew to head out to a club, a Monte Carlo passed by. Jimmy flashed his trademark smirk, and the car stopped, looked at us, and then peeled out. I was like, "What the fuck?" I knew that it was going to be a problem that we had to solve.

A couple of hours later, our whole crew was standing on the corner when the Monte Carlo pulled up and stopped. Five guys got out. They all looked familiar, but I didn't know them by name.

The biggest guy—naturally—came over and asked, "Who's Jimmy?"

Before Jimmy could say anything, I jumped in and said, "I'm Jimmy. What's your problem?"

The guy said he wanted to know why I was laughing at his friends before and that he was "handling it for them now."

Then, this pipsqueak with him chimes in, "You don't want to make Vinny angry, because Vinny gets *violent*." I felt like I was in an episode of *The Honeymooners* when the guy in the pool hall says to Ralph Kramden, "You don't want to make Harvey mad."

Anyway, I started mimicking the kid's voice, saying, "Oh, I guess I don't want to make Violent Vinny mad then!" I picked up a bicycle that was laying on the sidewalk and walked up to Violent Vinny with it. I told him, "I'm gonna throw this bike onto the telephone pole, and you're gonna follow it." I had no idea what the fuck I was saying. It sounded so stupid, but I was so convincing. They cursed us out, piled back into the car, and took off.

Years later, I heard that Vinny was doing five years for assault and battery. Who would've thought a nice guy like that would end up in prison, huh?

These stories seem endless. Back then, you had to puff up your feathers just to survive the constant attacks in the neighborhood. I was a short kid, but I worked out, bulked up, and became very strong for my size. Over time, I developed a reputation for being a bit crazy after a few fights and verbal abuse with some shady characters.

One of those characters was Gino Lungo. Gino was hanging out on 14th Avenue and 86th Street one night with a group of his friends. They were rising stars in the Bonanno family.

Rob and I were waiting for the light at that corner, hysterically laughing at a joke I'd just told him, and Gino approached our car.

He asked, "What the fuck are you laughing at?" and then, without warning, punched Rob in the face! Most of the kids from the neighborhood were paranoid narcissists who thought everyone was talking about them, so this wasn't all that surprising.

I took off and headed back to our hangout, gathering about twenty guys to back me up. I was furious, but now I felt empowered because I had backup. We piled into five cars and drove back to 14th Avenue, pulling up like it was a raid.

When I started approaching Gino, he got into a car and locked the door. I pounded on the window and told him, "Get the fuck out of the car!" I watched too many movies as a kid because I had no business doing that. The driver took off, and I thought I'd squashed that beef—but I was wrong.

A couple of weeks after the Gino Lungo incident, I was waiting by the payphone on the corner of 16th and Bath Avenues. Back then, you'd wait by the payphone for calls from your friends to find out where they were and how long they were going to be. Everyone had those payphone numbers memorized.

While I was waiting, a van pulled up, and four guys jumped out with baseball bats. It was Gino and his crew, here to settle up from the 14th Avenue incident. It felt surreal, but in that split second, I didn't run. I thought that if I ran, they'd have an easier time hitting me from behind with those bats than if I faced them. Then the driver stepped out of the van.

It was Steve Ferragamo. He walked right over to me, grinning, shook my hand, and said, "Wait a second, boys."

He said to them, "He's a good kid. He's got some pair of balls, ya know. We ain't doin' nothin' to him." They had been telling Ferragamo half-truths about what happened, conveniently forgetting the part where Gino had punched Rob in the face for no reason. Who knew that my paddleball game had helped me keep my pretty-boy good looks?

History repeated itself on 14th Avenue, though we didn't know it at the time. It was about 1 a.m., and the 4th of July fireworks were dying down, leaving a haze of smoke in the air. The faint smell of barn fires from neighborhood "displays" lingered, mixing with the night air. Everything in the neighborhood seemed to be quieting down, but we were about to stir up something much bigger.

Rob and I were driving home from watching fireworks light up the Bath Avenue sky. As we're talking at a red light, a Trans Am pulls up next to us. Rob's girlfriend is in the car with friends, and that's when Rob loses it!

He bolts out of the car, yanks open the passenger door, and tells his girlfriend to get the fuck outta the car! The male driver, clearly confused, doesn't know what the hell is happening, so he takes off with the door still wide open. Jane was still inside. When he turns the corner, the door slams shut after it hits a parked car.

Rob jumps back into the car, and the chase is on! I'm yelling at him to forget it and let's just go home, but he's not hearing it. We tail them all the way to the golf course, where they finally pull over. Jane runs out of the car, and she and Rob start arguing in the street.

Then this huge Puerto Rican guy in a silk button-down shirt gets out of his car and walks over to ours. I start scanning for something to hit him with, but there's nothing.

He rips open his shirt right in front of me and said, "First I'm gonna kill your buddy, and then I'm comin' to kill you!"

I'm freaking out, so I grab my car keys, slip them between my fingers, and catch up to this lunatic. He spins around without hesitation and roundhouses me in the face. I go down like a bag of potatoes, but I pop right back up because the pain hasn't set in... yet.

Meanwhile, Rob's still arguing with his girlfriend, oblivious to what's going on. I jump on this guy's back, lock one arm around his throat, and start hammering him in the back of the head with my keys. But it's not doing much—well, it's not doing anything except pissing him off more.

Rob still doesn't notice I'm struggling to take down this guy while he's busy berating his girlfriend. I'm screaming for him to help me get this cock sucker to the ground. It's not long before the guy starts slamming me against the fence with me on his back.

Finally, he yells to his friend, "Get the ax!" Exhausted, I fall to the ground, and Rob finally snaps out of it. We run for the car with his girlfriend in tow. Rob fumbles with the ignition, and all we hear is the squeal of our car trying to start, but it won't. I thought this only happens in horror movies!

The lumberjack was running toward us with his ax in hand, and I yelled at Rob to start the fucking car. Meanwhile, Rob was screaming at his girlfriend, jealousy clouding his mind. As you can see, this wasn't going well. Then, just as the guy got close, the car finally roared to life—Vroom! Vroom!

Before the first swing can land, we peeled out of there and head straight to Gary's house. The numbness in my jaw is wearing off, and the pain is starting to hit me. We just dodged a bullet—or, more accurately, an ax. That week, Rob made his father sell that piece of junk, and we got through another situation together.

We loved to bowl when axes weren't part of the scene. It was huge in the '80s. There were bowling allies every few blocks, and they were always packed. One of our regular spots was on 18th Avenue and Benson.

One night, we were getting ready to head home around 11 p.m. As we passed through the green light, a car ran the red and T-boned us. Luckily, no one was hurt, but the car was smashed. I got out of the car, and the kid who hit us took off down Benson Avenue.

For some reason, I thought I could catch up with a speeding car, so I started running after it. What in God's earth made me think I could catch a speeding car? I gave up pretty quickly and went back to the bowling alley to call my dad.

He showed up, just as this guy Sally Black did. Sally owned a used car lot down the street. Believe it or not, he was connected. He walked over to my dad and said his kid brother was the driver. Not only had he stolen the car from his lot, but he didn't even have a driver's license.

I mouthed off to Sally a bit, and my dad had to calm me down. He never saw that side of me before. He only knew me as the altar boy and Eagle Scout. Sally handed my father $1200 in cash and told him to take the car to a body shop his friend owned, with instructions not to put it through insurance. The car was fixed in less than a week, complete with an interior steam cleaning to boot.

A few weeks after things calmed down with the car accident, me and Jimmy went to the Vegas Diner for some cheeseburgers. It was the ultimate hangout. It felt like the middle of the afternoon, even though it was 4 a.m., because after a night of clubbing, everyone headed there for breakfast, or like us, a very late dinner. As I mentioned before, Jimmy's brother Al was connected to a crime family. He was low on the totem pole, but he got into trouble with the wrong people and had to go on the run.

While we were sitting in the booth, Nicky Corallo came over. I didn't know Nicky personally, and I didn't want to. If you knew him, it was only a matter of time before you ended up either dead or in prison.

He walked up to our table and said, "Hey Jimmy, I've been looking for your brother. Where is he?" Jimmy told him his brother had just left home and that he had no idea where he was. Nicky lifted his shirt, showing a gun, and said, "Well, when you talk to him, tell him I'm lookin' for him."

Jimmy was physically shaking by the time Nicky walked away. You see, he was a known hitman in the neighborhood. He'd later go to prison for the assassination of a couple of wise guys. Jimmy knew his brother was in deep because they were good friends—and now it didn't seem like Nicky was going to be inviting Jimmy's brother over for Christmas dinner anytime soon.

We paid the bill, which was a rarity when I went to diners, and left. Jimmy threw up the whole cheeseburger deluxe meal when we got to the car. If I'd known, I would have made sure he took it to go so it wouldn't be wasted on the side of the street.

Turns out, Jimmy's brother owed money or was stealing from the profits. You can't mess around with people like that. They don't give you a tongue-lashing or report you to the cops. They handle things their way, and trust me, it's not a ride on the Starship Enterprise. Jimmy's brother was in and out of trouble his whole life, but eventually, he got his act together—far, far away in another state.

Chapter 8

Lovers' Lanes, Jocks, and College Days

How many times have you been to a lover's lane? Come on, don't be shy. You didn't go all the way, or you just sat there talking, but you definitely had the experience. If a girl went there often, it meant her boyfriend was a cheap bastard. We had plenty of places to park in the neighborhood for a little backseat action.

I had a couple of incidents—once, a guy climbed a tree and was watching us through my sunroof! You've got to be pretty desperate to climb 20 feet up onto a limb just to get your kicks. Another time, me and Rob were with two girls from Staten Island, and the car got stuck in the mud. We called a tow truck, and that was the end of those two girls.

Rob used to go to Marine Park with his girlfriend. One night, he came back to our hangout all pissed. He said there was a guy who always parked next to them just to leer into their car. He was fed up and wanted us to teach the guy a lesson. He came up with a plan for our crew to go over and egg the guy's car. We bought a few dozen eggs and set off on our mission at about midnight.

Rob told us it was a red car but couldn't remember the make or model. He pointed to a red Corvette and said, "That's it." So, we hatched (get it?) a plan to circle the car and egg it all at once. We snuck up and surrounded the car. Rob gave the signal, and we bombarded it with eggs. We expected the guy to take off, but we made a big mistake.

He not only stayed, but he also stepped out of the car. And let me tell you, this guy was massive. It seemed like he had to unfold himself to get out. We'd picked the wrong car! This dude was with his girlfriend, and we totally ruined their moment. He yelled something at us, but it wasn't even a coherent sentence.

We scattered like cockroaches in the dark winter park at midnight, fleeing a blue-balled psycho. I ran into the basketball courts, which were all fenced in, and I couldn't find an exit. Then, Blue-Balls comes into the courts. I couldn't see him too well, but I sure as hell could hear his heavy breathing.

I had to think fast, so I started doing jumping jacks. Here I am, in the middle of the night, wearing a furry-hooded parka... exercising? I was counting out the reps out loud so he could hear. Can you believe this dumb fuck just passed me by and went back out the way he came in? Who's going to think someone's mimicking Jack LaLanne in a pitch-black park at 25 degrees? Eventually, we all met up and staked out the lot until Blue-Balls left with his butt-ugly girlfriend.

A few months after the egg toss, we started hanging out at a club on Staten Island. It was our comfort zone because everyone was from Staten Island, so we could let our hair down. Madonna was performing there one night before she got famous. The place was packed with people from both Brooklyn and Staten Island.

Before Madonna performed, the crowd started spilling out into the parking lot, Staten Island guys on one side and Brooklyn guys on the other. We didn't want to get involved with any shenanigans, because we didn't have a beef with anyone. Before you could say Verrazzano-Narrows Bridge, the two groups collided!

I didn't know whether to shit or go blind, but I found myself right in the middle of the fight, with everyone I went with split up. I saw this poor kid get thrown in front of a moving van like a rag doll. His body was completely run over, and I never found out what happened to him.

I looked up and saw Gary, and we just started running. We heard gunshots as we ran to the next block and hid behind a car until we felt it was safe. Then we started walking... and walking, until we met these kids from Brooklyn who gave us a ride to our car. They were bragging about the fight and how they had won. Jesus, we were in way over our heads. I heard it made the Staten Island Advance newspaper, but I never wanted to know what happened because I missed my one and only chance to see Madonna before she became famous!

The whole incident at the club was a mess, and it was clear we needed something a little less chaotic to fill our time. So, we figured we'd try something "safe"— a Touch Football league. No fights, no guns... just healthy fun and some running around, right? Well, it wasn't quite as simple as we thought.

Me and the guys, who weren't exactly the tallest trees in the forest, decided to form a team. Can you believe there was an ambulance stationed at the field every Sunday for the games? The brawls between teams and the rough play kept them busy. We hardly ever won a game, but we sure got into plenty of fights on the field.

There was one thing that was worse than the fighting for us as a team—Jock Itch! My crotch started to itch, and it kept getting worse. I was putting powder down there to no avail. I call Rob, and he tells me the same thing! We were never with the same girl, so it can't be that. We found out one by one—the entire team had jock itch.

Finally, we figured it out: it was the new uniform pants we bought for the games. To join, all you needed was jerseys, but we figured it was better to look good than to be good, so we got pants too. Jerry, who worked part-time in a pharmacy, bought us jock itch cream that cured the burn and itching, but it didn't cure our case of the dropsies on the football field. We were masochists, signing up for the league year after year.

I have to say, we had spunk, but we lacked height and true ability. The other teams stacked their rosters with ringers who played college ball, all to vie for the championship. We kept showing up and giving it our all. While we couldn't compete with the bigger and better teams, the laughs on the field made it all worth it.

Whether it was the fights on the field or the jock itch going around the team, we just couldn't catch a break. So, we figured we'd hit up Wildwood for a weekend. Meet some girls, hang out on the beach, and go clubbing. But, of course, like always, it didn't exactly go the way we planned.

Wildwood, New Jersey, was a hot spot for college kids. Me and the boys decided to head down for Memorial Day Weekend, but it was wild with no wood. We didn't reserve motel rooms, nor did we know how to get there. So, we packed our bags, went to a gas station for a street map (yes, an actual street map), and marked out our route. None of us had really driven that far from home yet.

When we looked at the map, we saw the Goethals Bridge that goes from Staten Island to New Jersey. We'd been on that bridge a million times, so we kept looking for roads that led to Wildwood from there. Rob showed us that Route 9 goes all the way from the bridge down to Wildwood. He's a genius—except for one thing: it's a local road filled with traffic lights, not a highway!

Instead of a trip that should have taken 2.5 hours, it took us over 8 hours. We were exhausted by the time we reached our first motel. It was 2 a.m., and the night manager wasn't too happy to see us. We should've known this wasn't the place to stay after he handed us pillows to bring to the room.

We opened the door, and it reeked of shit. No blankets in sight and the sheets looked like prostitutes had been rolling around on them for the last month without washing. Jerry said we should just lay our beach towels on the beds and go to sleep, but Gary was pissed that we didn't meet any girls within the first ten minutes of being in town at 2 a.m. The bugs running around in the bathroom seemed to wink at me when I told everyone we should just sleep in the car, so we left.

Morning came, and we decided to head back home to lick our wounds. But how do we get back? Route 9 of course! The same stupid road back to NYC. Rob suggested Six Flags, and somehow, everyone swore it was just down the road. Seven hours later, we finally made it! It wasn't Wildwood, but we got some food, met a few girls, and made the best of it.

In the late '80s, our crew made our yearly spring break trek to Fort Lauderdale, Florida. There were wet t-shirt contests, guys turning over rent-a-cars, and chugging beer through funnels—it was nuts. Sometimes, we'd even go down twice a year because we were having so much fun watching this shit.

We met a group of rich Arab American girls from Michigan one year and hung out with them all week. We played tricks on them the whole time. They hid cash in their room, thinking we'd never find it. I lifted the rug by the window, and there it was (a little-known trick). Between picking bathroom locks while they showered and uncovering their stash, we definitely won them over as friends.

One night, Jimmy was in their room when the phone rang. He picked it up, and a guy on the other end asked who he was. Thinking it was me, Jimmy said, "We're hanging out with the Arab girls tonight."

The guy dropped the phone, and we found out he was one of their boyfriends back home. He immediately jumped in his Corvette and sped down to Florida from Michigan, getting arrested in Ohio for driving 120 mph.

That same night, I met a girl at the club and walked her back to her hotel. Like a gentleman, I left her at the front door—though maybe she just rebuffed my innuendos about coming upstairs. I called my hotel room, and the boys were already paired off with the Arabs. It was late, I was tired, and my room was occupied by the United Nations, so I ended up sleeping on the front lawn of the Holiday Inn. It might've been the best sleep of my life! I woke up rested and ready for the next Wet T-Shirt contest.

Because we always had a blast on vacation, me, Gary, and our buddy Lenny decided to book a spontaneous, all-inclusive resort trip to the Bahamas. Now, you know Gary, he was always a guy in heat. I told him to take it easy, reminding him that we had a whole week ahead of us. So, we headed down to the beach, looking to soak up some sun.

As we lounged in our beach chairs, taking it easy, a guy renting out jet skis came up and asked if we wanted to give it a try. I told him maybe later, not wanting to interrupt our relaxation time. Well, wouldn't you know it, he went over to these two girls we didn't even realize were lying behind us, and asked them the same thing.

Turns out, these ladies were New Yorkers too. They told the guy, "The only way we're goin' on jet skis is if those two guys come with us." Now, me and Gary, being the oblivious buffoons that we were, never even considered they were talking about us. So, he taps us on the shoulder and asks if we want to change our minds and go with these lovely ladies. Before he even finished his sentence, Gary and I were on our feet, flexing a little muscle, and introduced ourselves to Dawn and Marie, who turned out to be from Queens.

We hit it off right away, laughing our way through the quick safety training session (if you want to call it that) and hopping on the jet skis, with Dawn on mine and Marie on Gary's. We set out, feeling the rush of the waves beneath us as we sped across the water. It was pure exhilaration, with the wind in our hair and the sun kissing our skin—and hopefully, them kissing us later on.

Naturally, since you guys already know a little about my life, this couldn't end well. As luck would have it, things took a turn for the worse. Dawn kept leaning the wrong way as I made turns, causing the jet ski to capsize—not once, but multiple times! There we were, bobbing in the ocean, gasping for breath amid fits of laughter. And as I clung to my life jacket (since I couldn't swim), I looked out into the distance to see Gary and Marie gracefully gliding through the waves, totally oblivious to our situation.

Getting desperate, Dawn and I waved frantically, trying to catch their attention. They spotted us and drove over to help, trying to flip it back upright. We were screwed because the jet ski had taken in water and was now flooded. So, Gary went to get help back at shore from the Bahama guys, who had a small boat just for these kinds of situations.

Now I'm totally embarrassed, waiting patiently to be plucked from the ocean. The smile has completely faded from Dawn's face, and frustration has set in. Here comes the Bahama guys to the rescue. As the boat gets closer, he cuts the engine and glides toward us, carefully trying to maneuver it so he can help us aboard.

It's getting closer and closer to me... I'm moving at a snail's pace to get to the side of the boat, but I miscalculated its speed, and now the boat has run me over. I can hear the gurgling sound of the Bahama guy yelling, "HE'S UNDER THE BOAT!"

The Bahama guy started the engine and with my eyes wide open, I saw the propeller start to turn and head straight for me! Suddenly, I was yanked by my vest—thankfully, the Bahama guy jumped in and saved me from the blades that would've turned me into sushi for the night's dinner.

As the boat chugged its way back to shore, I glanced over at Dawn. I thought she was ready to give me a piece of her mind. Her face was all scrunched up, and I could practically see the steam coming out of her ears. But, surprise-surprise, she actually walked over to me.

"Ya know," she said, carrying that unmistakable New York mouth, "I'm actually glad I didn't have to go home and tell my friends and family that I killed a guy on my first freakin' day of vacation!"

After that whole hullabaloo, we made it back to shore in one piece. We spent the rest of the week together, had a pretty good time, and, when we got home, we never spoke to each other again.

Back home, my college career was pretty close to overturning a jet ski. I bounced from one college to another, because nothing seemed right, you know what I'm saying?

My first stop was C.W. Post College in Long Island, NY. There was all this pressure that made me pack up my stuff and bounce after just a year. It was like that feeling when you realize the pizza's too greasy even for Brooklyn, and you just have to get out of there before it all goes south. Looking back, I'm glad I left, but it sure wasn't easy figuring out the next move.

So, get this, back in the day, they didn't bother asking you who you wanted as a roommate. Nah, they just tossed our applications up in the air like confetti, and wherever they landed, that was your roomie. And who did I end up with? I got George, a 375-pound African American offensive lineman, and Devin, this stereotypical Irish guy whose folks had enough cash to buy him a golden ticket into the school.

Now, picture this: I end up in the athletic dorm, surrounded by guys so big they must've been grown in factories. I felt like a fish out of water, swimming in a sea of jocks. And to make things worse, I found out the school was what they call a "suitcase school." Know what that means? Most of these kids lived just a hop, skip, and a jump away from the campus, so they'd pack their bags like they were heading to the Hamptons and bail out of there every weekend.

But let me dive back into the wild world of my roommates. First, there's George, this behemoth of a man. Not only was he huge, but he was big on cleanliness, too. This guy was takin' more showers than a mermaid in the Atlantic. Three showers a day, can you believe it? Now, you'd think that's a good thing, right? Freshness overload! But hold on, it wasn't all roses.

You ever try to share a tiny dorm bathroom with a guy who spends half his day under the showerhead? Let's just say, it wasn't exactly a spa day. Every time he stepped out, the whole room smelled like a department store, but it also felt like I was waiting forever for my turn. The whole thing was like living with a professional athlete who cared way too much about his hygiene. Honestly, I started wondering if the dude was secretly in training for the Cleanest Person in America competition.

So, here's how it went down: George would come back to the room after every shower, strutting around like he was the king of hygiene, and what'd he do? Drop his towel and start bullshitting with me, butt-naked, like we were just hanging out on the stoop, shooting the breeze. I couldn't unsee what I saw. It was like a front-row seat to the circus that I never asked for.

But wait, here's the real kicker. He had not one, but two roll-on deodorants. Yeah, you heard me right. One for his underarms, the usual stuff, but the other one? A special roll-on deodorant just for his butt crack. I kid you not. And you know what this guy would do? He'd plop his foot right up on my bed, like it was the most normal thing in the world, balls hanging lower than the

Brooklyn Bridge, and start rolling that deodorant up and down his crack like I wasn't even there.

I mean, c'mon, George! I'm just trying to get myself settled into college life, and here you are turning our dorm room into a naked spa session with extra deodorant. It was like a bizarre episode of The Real World—except there was no camera crew, just me trying not to make eye contact while my roommate treated my bed like a footstool. Every day, I'd sit there, trying to act like it wasn't happening, but honestly, it was impossible to ignore.

Devin, on the other hand, was quiet, like some kind of mysterious ghost, keeping to himself and disappearing whenever he felt like it. The guy lived just a stone's throw away from campus, so he wasn't at the dorm every night. But when he showed up, it was a whole different story. He'd stumble in, drunk as a skunk, clothes all disheveled like he'd just crawled out of a dumpster. And every time, without fail, he'd collapse right there in the middle of the room, passed out cold.

But hold on, it gets worse. In the middle of the night, out of nowhere, he'd shoot up like a zombie—no warning, no rhyme or reason—and start puking all over himself. You'd think, after making that mess, he'd have some decency to clean up, right? Nah. Instead, the guy would just curl back up like nothing happened and go right back to sleep. Puke-covered and all, like it was the most normal thing in the world. I'm sitting there in the dark, just thinking, "What the hell is this guy's deal?"

It happened one too many times, and by about 4 a.m., I couldn't take it anymore. I packed up my stuff and went back home, and I never came back to that dorm again. I wasn't about to stick around for Devin's next drunken performance. But you know what? It became one of those legendary stories you end up telling' your friends for years.

So yeah, my college journey definitely had some twists and turns, to say the least. After all that chaos, I moved on to St. John's University, where I spent my days hustling fellow students out of their tuition money, beating them at pool. Eventually, I ended up finishing up my college career at The College of Staten Island. A real ride if you ask me.

Chapter 9

You Gotta Be Kidding Me

You'd think all those situations in my younger years got me prepared for big moments in my adult life, but I don't think anything prepares you for cancer. That's exactly what I experienced years later as I was wheeled down the halls of a cancer center in NYC, headed for surgery. Anxiety gripped me tighter than a toddler holding onto his teddy bear.

As I was being wheeled in the hallway, I noticed all the abstract artwork that lined the walls. It seemed like they were trying to distract me, but trust me, it wasn't working. Just when I thought my nerves couldn't take anymore, this sharply dressed administrator appeared out of nowhere, shooing off the attendant like he was about to deliver a mob secret.

"Listen, we have a bit of a situation," he started, leaning in close, his voice just above a whisper. "It appears that you're not covered for this surgery."

I felt numb, "What?!" I said in disbelief. "How come I wasn't told about this sooner?"

He nodded slowly, with a smirk and comment about just following protocol. "I'm afraid your business partner wrote the insurance company a check that bounced. You see, we have strict policies..."

He paused like an attorney addressing the jury, "There's a chance, though. If your partner can get a new check directly to the insurance company's office within the next hour, we can proceed with the surgery."

I couldn't believe what I was hearing. This was a freakin' nightmare as usual! My brain started running wild, picturing Rizzo bolting through Manhattan like some kind of unfit superhero. I could see him ducking cabs, dodging tourists, and nearly taking out a pretzel cart while waving a check in the air. It was nuts, but so was my situation—lying on a gurney, waiting on a guy whose track record was shaky at best.

The administrator stood there, looking like he'd just delivered last rites, "No other option," he said, like this was just another Tuesday for him. No big deal, right? Just your life dangling on whether Rizzo could pull this off.

I forced a smile, even though I wanted to scream. "Guess I gotta trust Rizzo to get that check where it needs to go," I said, trying to keep it together. But trust? Ha! I knew better. I had no idea if he'd show up with a check.

As they wheeled me into the surgical room, I kept thinking, "*What kinda idiot ends up in a mess like this?*" My life was riding on Rizzo, and that didn't make me feel too confident.

And so, as the surgical team prepped their shiny tools and the anesthesiologist leaned in, ready to knock me out, all I could do was hope, pray, and chuckle. Only time would tell if Rizzo would pull off last-minute heroics, or if I'd end up on a gurney, in a street, in the middle of Manhattan. But, he got the check to the insurance company and they popped that cancer and some other shit right out of my body.

While I was recovering, voiceless from complications, I discovered a few months later that the check had bounced like a Super Ball in a schoolyard. I could've cried, but instead, I just sat there, emotionless, as the bills rolled in like a wave of linebackers dogpiling onto a fumble. Every envelope felt heavier than the last, like they were taunting me. I could already hear Rizzo's voice in my head, promising he'd take care of everything, but now I was stuck.

I started asking myself why the hell I let it get this far. I mean, I'm no dummy—I grew up on the streets and learned my lessons the hard way. But somehow, I let Rizzo and his bullshit drag me into this mess. I should have seen it coming. I should have been smart enough to sidestep this disaster before it battered me— just another car hitting me like in the old days.

I stared out my window, thinking about all the times I'd let Rizzo's bullshit slide. Enough was enough. I had to cut ties, no more excuses. It was time to start fresh, leave him behind like a broken-down jalopy on the Belt Parkway, and finally take control of my own life.

Chapter 10

Twisted Balls

During my life, doctors have always been tinkering with my body parts. As an adult, it was cancer, but in my early 20s, it was twisted balls—Ouchy Mama! From time to time during puberty and beyond, I had this unbearable pain in my balls that would go away after a few minutes or, at most, a couple of hours. I always figured it was just from "straining myself" while playing sports. I never really told anyone about it—too embarrassing to talk about pain in my testicles! This went on for years, and I just saw it as another hurdle in life I had to jump over.

One night, I came home around 11 p.m. after some long racquetball games. My parents were deep in their 11th dream by then, so I tried to creep around the apartment, not wanting to wake them up. I took a quick shower and practically passed out on my bed.

No sooner than you can say "twisted," I woke up with this excruciating pain in my balls. I couldn't even let my clothes touch them because it hurt so much, so I stripped down and lay on the floor with my legs spread eagle for a couple of hours. I was praying to God for some relief, but at the same time, I was thinking, if God didn't respond, what was I gonna do?

I dragged myself into the bathroom, got some Bengay, put a little on my finger, and massaged it into my balls. Yeah, you can imagine where this is going. My balls started shrinking and burning like two toasted marshmallows. I couldn't scream because I didn't want to wake my parents. So, I grabbed a washcloth, soaked it in cold water, and started the long Bengay removal process. But the pain still wasn't going away. I had to take desperate measures.

I crawled to my parents' room, naked, in the dark. I pulled myself up to the side of their bed and tapped my mother on the shoulder. I said, "I got a pain in my testicles, and Dad needs to take me to the hospital."

She just rolled over to Dad, casually, and said, "Can you get up and see what's wrong with Richie's balls?" Thinking about it now, she must've been asleep because if your son wakes you up in the middle of the night and says his balls hurt, you don't just roll over like that!

Anyway, Dad started getting dressed like he's heading to work. I thought he was gonna start shaving too! I said, "Dad, we gotta go now! Just grab me some sweatpants and let's get movin'!"

Finally, it clicked—he sees his 22-year-old son, naked, in pain. My parents helped me get some sweats on, and we headed out to the car. Dad asks, "What hospital do you wanna go to?" At that point, I'm like, "Does it really matter? I've been in pain for over 4 hours now. Just take me anywhere!"

We got to the hospital, and the triage nurse could see I'm in agony, so she called an emergency room nurse to examine me. Normally, I wouldn't mind a woman feeling my nuts, but this time? Big exception to the rule.

The second she touched them, I started banging my head against the wall and screaming in pain. Thank God for that nurse, though; she knew exactly what was going on.

Testicular Torsion. Here's the dictionary explanation: "It happens when the spermatic cord, which provides blood flow to the testicle, twists and cuts off the blood supply, causing sudden pain and swelling. Testicular torsion requires surgery right away to save the testicle." My definition? It's like getting kicked in the balls by a fuckin' horse... period.

As they prepped me for surgery, in walked a guy dressed in pajamas and sneakers. He was my new surgeon and best friend, Dr. Franklin. He started asking me a bunch of questions, but then suddenly stopped, turned to my mother, and said, "These are personal questions I need to ask your son. Can you give us some privacy, please?"

Privacy? From my mother? This guy was out of his mind if he thinks she's not going to be within earshot for this. I swear, I could still hear her breathing outside the curtain when he asked me if I was sexually active. Next thing I know, the curtain goes taut like a sailboat catching a northeast wind! My mom must've grabbed it from the other side so she wouldn't fall down. I think I even saw the silhouette of her Rosary beads catching fire!

He then told me a bit about the surgery and what could go wrong. After that, he had me sign paperwork saying they might have to lop off one or both of my balls.

What the fuck?? I had questions I needed answers to, but there was no time.

Finally, they wheeled me into surgery, and I was left under the blinding overhead lights with just my anxieties and a fading image of Mom's face, looking like she might faint.

Next thing I knew, I woke up in recovery with a nurse standing over me, her face all calm as she said, "The surgery went well."

I blink, still disoriented, and then it hits me—the first question rushes to the surface. "Did you... were you able to... save both?"

The nurse chuckled softly and nodded. "Yes, everything's intact."

Relief flooded over me like a tidal wave. I sneaked a peek under the sheets, half-expecting *No-balls Richie*, but thank God, that's not what I got. My balls were resting in a sling with a hole for, well, my peesh to poke through. It looks straight out of a dungeon in medieval times, like some weird piece of S&M gear. But hey, if that's what it takes to keep everything where it belongs, I'll take it. The world is right again.

Chapter 11

The Job that Never Went Out of Style

Back when I was looking for some extra cash during college, Rob's dad caught wind of someone needing part-time help and asked if I wanted the guy's number. The company? Endless Allure Originals. The owner? A guy named Luigi—of course, it had to be an Italian guy, right? They specialized in junior sportswear—clothes a young girl would wear to look good for a night, only for it to shrink in the wash and vanish from her closet just as fast.

So, I gave Luigi a call the next day and mentioned I was a friend of Rob's and was looking for a gig. He told me to come by that afternoon and gave me the address. It wasn't far—just a couple of miles from my place.

When I showed up, it was one of those nondescript storefronts you'd pass by a hundred times without even noticing. I knocked on the locked door, and there he was: a smooth, middle-aged guy with a full head of silver hair, looking like he had just stepped out of Bensonhurst Quarterly Magazine.

He gave me a once-over and said, "Richie?" I nodded, and he grinned. "You're hired. I can tell you're a good Italian boy—that Christ head around your neck says it all."

I had this gold Christ head pendant, the kind of thing everyone in Brooklyn had back then. It was a beauty—probably set my parents back a few car payments, but hey, worth it.

I started the job right away after my morning classes at college. Luigi introduced me to his wife, Maria, who had fiery red bouffant hair and makeup to match—everything about her made a statement. From the start, this couple's fashion sense was friggin' bold and unapologetically over the top. They were the stereotypical Italian couple with some money to spend—and spend they did!

My responsibilities included sweeping, mopping, packing boxes, and handwriting the packing slips that went with store orders. Maria looked at the slips like I printed them off a computer, the handwriting was that neat. I have to admit, my penmanship was on point! She noticed too, and before long, she had me update all the accounting ledgers, impressed by the care I took with every line. This became my foot in the door for bigger responsibilities, and I found myself getting more and more involved in the business.

I loved every minute of it—the pulse of the fashion world flowing through each style, coming to life from rolls of fabric and carefully picked chachkas. I felt like I was on the front lines of fashion, always ahead of the season's new colors and trends and getting a real sense of the artistry behind each piece.

One day, I walked into work, and Luigi flung this little green book onto the counter and said, "You're our new salesman. Start drumming up some business. Make appointments from this book."

Just like that. I flipped through page after page—all these companies, contact names, phone numbers—a sea of potential clients. I was eighteen, still in college, and here I was, thrown into the deep end with no clue about selling, who was I supposed to be selling to, or what the hell was I even supposed to say when I finally got one of these people on the phone.

My first few calls, I was leaving messages with the receptionist—real old-school style. Back then, there were no answering machines. You actually had to talk to a live person, usually some receptionist who'd scribble your message on a little slip of paper and leave it on the desk of whoever you were trying to reach. It was a whole different ball game. If you wanted to get through to someone, you needed a little charm, a lot of persistence, and a prayer that your note wouldn't get lost in the pile.

So, I got to this company that owned 250 stores across the country, a name I've heard of—Jane Lilly. I asked the receptionist to speak to the guy whose name was in the book—Nathan Abrams. I wasn't expecting much, just another voice message, but to my surprise, he actually picked up the phone! And on top of that, he's the first one to pick up for me so far.

So here I was, voice cracking, barely keeping it together, and as soon as I introduced myself, he said, "Richie, if you don't mind me asking, how old are you?"

I told him, "Eighteen." He started laughing and said, "I knew it! Kid, you got some pair of balls. Can you bring some samples over to my office in Moonachie, NJ tomorrow?" I was like, "Yes! Absolutely!"

Turns out, Nathan Abrams wasn't just some buyer. He was the actual owner of Jane Lilly. And somehow, I managed to get straight through to him.

When I told Luigi, his eyes went wide. He's been trying to get in with Jane Lilly for years and couldn't believe I somehow got a foot in the door. He didn't waste any time. He headed to the sample room, grabbed a bunch of new samples, and gave me the quickest crash course you can imagine—names of each piece, types of fabric, and a price list that was all shoved into a suitcase that barely zipped. Then he handed me directions to Moonachie scribbled on a ripped-up piece of paper, coffee stains and all, and told me to call him from a payphone if I needed anything. Need anything?? I thought I needed more than that, I needed a fuckin' miracle!

When I got to their office, I was greeted by a security guard who walked me through hallways lined with samples—dresses, tops, bottoms—that were fresh styles ready for the stores. There was a big conference room where fit models were trying on the latest styles, and the whole setup made me feel like I was way out of my league.

Finally, I got to Mr. Abrams' office. He was this older, Jewish guy with a gentle vibe, but you could tell he was totally in charge. He asked if I wanted a Coke, and then actually got it himself and poured it in a glass with ice. That small gesture totally put me at ease and made me feel like I actually belonged there.

This guy knew more about the styles in my bag than I did! He had a few girls try on some pieces, giving each one the once-over like he'd been doing this his whole life. Then, without breaking a sweat, he jotted down an order—3000 pieces that covered a few assorted styles, and said, "This'll be a sample order."

A sample order! My head was spinning. He looked at me and said he was impressed with how I handled myself, wanted to give me a shot, and on top of that, the styles were exactly what he was looking for.

He helped me pack up my bag, gave me a tour of the warehouse like I was part of his team, and then showed me out to my car. Before I knew it, we were shaking hands, and I was on my way. Honestly, it's one of those moments you don't forget, and he was one of the nicest guys I ever met in the business, who just happened to be my very first client.

I hit the first payphone I found at a gas station and called Luigi. I laid it all out for him, and you could practically hear his mind racing over the phone.

He told me, "Give me the styles and amounts they ordered." By the time I made it back to the office, he'd already placed the fabric order and started working on the patterns. Just like that, I had a whole new arsenal for my career path, and I was falling in love with the fashion business.

The business kept growing, getting bigger and bigger, and before long, we had to leave Brooklyn behind. Luigi bought this huge building in Staten Island, right by the expressway. It needed a ton of work to turn it into a fashion studio and warehouse, but Maria—well, she took charge.

She transformed the place into something straight out of Barbie's Dream House. The walls were painted pale pink, even the floors. You'd never seen a warehouse so chic. The offices had custom furniture everywhere, totally over the top. You couldn't miss the warehouse from the expressway, except Luigi wanted to keep it low-key because he didn't want to bring attention to it, especially from the mob. He had electronic gates put up with a speakerphone system—nobody could get in without being cleared first. No signage outside, either. They didn't need nosy neighbors catching a glimpse of what was going on and running their mouths.

Although I put in long days, it was a fun job at Endless Allure. One night, after one of those marathon shifts, I was shooting the breeze with Freddie Marchenetti, our production manager, out in the parking lot. Typical conversation with Freddie, yapping about the Mets and how they could actually do it this year. We must've been out there for a good hour—so long the sun started going down. Finally, we called it a night, said our goodbyes, and headed home.

The neighborhood our building was in wasn't Todt Hill, that's for sure. It was your classic industrial area that had warehouses and homes looking like they'd need a bulldozer soon. But you don't think about that stuff when you're just trying to get home. So, there I was, driving along, windows down, waiting for the air conditioning to kick in and cool me off.

I pulled up to a red light under the expressway that had big concrete pillars, dim lights, and a whole movie vibe. And out of nowhere—FUCK!—this guy came at the car like a cat and shoved a gun right through my window. "Leave your fuckin' wallet on the seat and get the fuck outta the car!" he snapped. My heart was pounding, and I couldn't even get a look at the guy. I froze for a second because all I could see in my peripheral vision was the gun pointed at my head.

I tried to stay calm like I'm Clint Eastwood in *Dirty Harry* or something. "Okay, okay," I told him, and I started leaning over to grab my wallet. But then something snapped inside me, and I just slammed my foot on the gas! The car roared forward, and the guy barely got his arm out of the window in time. I flew through the red light like Mario Andretti, not a thought about the cross traffic.

Four blocks later, I finally pulled over, shaking so badly I couldn't keep my hands still. I was sitting there, sobbing like a little kid, trying to make sense of what the hell just went down. My heart was pounding in my chest.

People always ask me, "How the hell did you have the balls to just drive off like that?" And honestly, I don't know. It wasn't balls at all. It was instincts kicked in, and thank God they did, because I had no idea what would've happened if I had stepped out of that car, but there was no question I wasn't sticking around to find out.

Getting back into the car after that was no easy task because my nerves were completely shot. Like an idiot, I didn't report it to the police. I figured they wouldn't do much, or maybe I just didn't want to deal with the hassle.

But then a couple of weeks later, I heard about a woman who was shot in a parking lot by a carjacker. That news hit me hard, and I felt so bad for her. It haunts me to this day. Every time I hear about something like that, I can't help but wonder, if I had just spoken up, could I have prevented it? The guy would've been caught before he hurt someone else. Who knows?

My company always used our own trucks for deliveries. There were a few reasons for that, but the biggest one was that if you start using those mobbed-up trucking services, you're done. They own you from the get-go. Once you're in their pocket, you're fucked. They have a way of making sure you can't get out.

Our trucks would pull right into the building, no questions asked, so outsiders never saw what was going on inside the warehouse. It was a small and safe bubble. You'd be surprised what businesspeople had to do back then to keep their hard-earned money for themselves. The whole system was rigged against you, and you either played by their rules or got left behind.

I liked to give people a chance to make a living, and I had a buddy whose brother-in-law came to me for a job. The guy had just gotten off drugs and booze and was desperate for a shot at redemption. So, I went to Luigi, explained the situation, and he said, "Alright, but if we hire him, he's all on you." So, I put him on the trucks to deliver garments to the stores.

The guy was a go-getter, no question. He was putting in the work, making twice as many trips as any other driver. I felt good about helping him out and bringing someone into the company who knew how to hustle. I thought I was doing the right thing by giving him a chance, you know? Until suddenly, he wasn't.

It started coming to the dispatcher's attention that dozens of garments were mysteriously vanishing from his deliveries. The losses started racking up into the thousands, and I was like, "What the hell is goin' on?"

The dispatcher came to me, out of courtesy, and asked how I wanted to handle it. I told him Luigi made this guy my responsibility, so I'd take care of it. Turns out, the driver had started using drugs again. And like an idiot, he thought he could cover it up by stealing the clothes to fund his habit.

I went to Luigi, laid it out, and he told me straight up, "Fire him on the spot, no pay, and we don't press charges." Simple as that.

When I called the driver to break the news, he wasn't happy about not getting paid. He shouted, "I'm comin' in to get my check." And I just knew it was going to turn into a fuckin' headache. I could see it happening.

Before he arrived, I told everyone in the office, "When he pulls into the lot, close the gates, lock the doors, and let me deal with him in the parking lot. Whatever happens out there, don't come out, and don't call the cops." I'd handle it. Simple as that. Man, did I make a fuckin' mistake.

The driver showed up, fuming like a bull on steroids. First thing out of his mouth? "Rich, get the fuck outta my way because I'm gettin' my check from Luigi." I stood my ground and told him straight up he wasn't getting it. That's when the gates started closing behind him with a loud *clang*.

His face turned as red as a firetruck, and he growled, "I don't wanna hurt you, so move!" When I didn't budge, he grabbed me by my shoulders and tried to shove me aside. His elbow hit me square in the face, and I saw stars. This wasn't the time to hum "Twinkle, Twinkle, Little Star" as he flung me straight into the boss's brand-new Mercedes. The dent had an imprint of my ass. Did I mention the guy was 6'3" and 260 pounds? Yeah, I didn't have a chance.

I started yelling, waving, doing everything I could to get someone to help. I looked up, and there's the whole company watching through the window. Just like I told them to do, *stay put*!

Finally, Luigi tosses a check out of the window and opens the gate. Bruised and exhausted from being tossed around like a rag doll, the driver left me to lick my wounds and snatched the check. He stumbled out, and that was the last I ever saw of him. Word on the street was, after all that mess, he was selling thousands of pieces of merchandise for like 50 bucks. What a sin.

When I wasn't getting tossed around, though, that job was the best I ever had. Most of the employees were Luigi and Maria's family. There was never a dull moment working there. That family could write a book about themselves, and it'd be a bestseller. Each one of them had their quirks, and each brought their own brand of wackiness to the place.

Luigi was the tough, no-nonsense boss. He was the stereotypical garment center guy, always yelling at somebody. He played the blame game, but underneath all that, he had a soft side, too. Maria kept everything running smoothly and went out of her way to help anyone in need. She was more worried about buying gifts for people than showing up to work. And then there were their family members... each one had their own memorable stories, and some of them were famous around the office.

I can't express enough how much I loved that place and the people I worked with. But when the feds passed the free trade agreement, it turned everything upside down. The whole game changed. I had no choice but to step back, leave the industry I'd known for so long, and figure out a whole new path for myself. It wasn't easy, but I knew I had to roll with it and make it work.

Chapter 12

I Love Lisa

I was somewhere between careers and—if we're being honest—marriages, when I thought, "Hey, why not real estate?" It seemed like a decent way to pivot my life in a positive direction or at least a temporary escape from the chaos of divorce proceedings and trying to chart out my next steps. Plus, you know how it goes in New York: why have one career crisis when you can have three?

And, wouldn't you know it, I actually took to the business. In fact, I was doing pretty well! So, I decided to give back and donate a slice of my commissions to the American Cancer Society. I even did a little advertising around it—you know, a win-win situation. The ACS got some cash, and I got a nice little PR boost.

At one of their big charity events, I had the honor of handing over one of those classic oversized checks. They made a whole to-do of it, and I found myself standing up there, feeling surprisingly fancy. But I'll tell you, my moment in the spotlight was totally upstaged.

Out of nowhere, this four-year-old kid with leukemia took the microphone and absolutely stole the show. The ballroom was packed with New York's finest from the medical field—people who barely blink at five-figure donations—and here's this cute little warrior, bald from treatments, standing there in his black tux, giving the most inspiring speech I'd ever heard. He talked about the summer camp he attends for kids with cancer, how much he loves it, and why we should all be donating to keep it going.

I don't think I've ever seen wallets fly open that fast. This kid had people practically throwing checks onto the stage! When the evening wrapped up, I went up to him and told him how proud I was of him. He gave me this big grin—like he knew he'd worked the room better than anyone there.

So, naturally, I had to get the name of this pint-sized powerhouse. I asked him, "What's your name, bud?" Without missing a beat, he straightened his little tuxedo, looked me dead in the eye, and said, "Tommy," with all the swagger of a guy five times his age. I couldn't help but laugh—this kid was a charmer.

Then I thought, *"Well, who raised this superstar?"* So, I asked him if his parents were around. He looked up, shrugged, and said, "My dad doesn't come to these things, but my mom is over there." He pointed across the room, and when I turned to look, it was like the entire place faded into soft focus.

Standing there was this stunning woman in a sexy black gown that flowed over every curve like it was painted on. She had these striking green eyes flecked with gold, which were absolutely mesmerizing. In that instant, I knew two things: I was done for, and little Tommy was my ticket to go chat with her.

I looked back at him and thought, "*This kid already stole the show tonight... what's one more act?*" So, with two huge goofy grins, Tommy and I approached his mom. She was standing next to another boy, all decked out like a miniature male model—his older brother, Frankie.

Tommy introduced me like a pro, all serious, saying, "This is my new friend, Richie," as if he were doing me the biggest favor of my life. Before I knew it, I was chatting with his mom—this incredible, fierce woman with an effortless smile.

She told me she was a hairstylist, working Sundays at the salon to keep some cash flowing while spending the rest of her week single-handedly managing Tommy's care. You could tell right away she was juggling a lot but handling it like a total pro.

And what a stroke of luck—I've got hair in need of a cut now and then!

Curious, I asked about her husband, and she let out this little sigh. Turns out, they were mid-divorce. She explained, with a calm fire in her eyes, that caring for Tommy had given her incredible confidence. If she could handle this on her own, she could handle anything.

And, in classic Staten Island style, she'd told her husband she was leaving him while he was eating a Big Mac and fries.

Right then, it hit me—I was talking to someone exceptional, a woman juggling life's curveballs with humor, resilience, and style. Lisa's straightforwardness was refreshing. Unlike anyone else I'd met, she had this knack for speaking her mind, even when I didn't expect it. And, yes, she was gorgeous, too.

I thought, "*Cha-ching! This woman is a gem,*" and little Tommy and his older brother Frankie were just the icing on the cake. I knew I loved Lisa when I saw how beautifully she raised her boys and how she treated me with total respect. Her kindness to me and others was very cool, and you could see her strength was unquestionable.

Never one to let a golden opportunity slip through my fingers, I took a breath, put on my best Matthew

McConaughey voice, and said, "Would you mind if I got your number or email? You know, just to keep in touch."

She laughed, thinking I had some nerve, but she scribbled them down with a grin that told me I'd managed to make a decent impression.

As soon as I got home, I ran straight to the laptop, and there she was, already online, like she somehow knew I'd be logging on, ready to find her.

Now, for all you youngsters out there, back in the day, we had AOL Instant Messenger. You'd log on, scroll through that little list of friends, and hope to catch someone online. Well, that night, I was the lucky one.

So, there we were, chatting away over Instant Message, and before I knew it, the hours had vanished. By around 4 a.m., fueled by pure impulse and a little insomnia, I worked up the nerve to ask if she'd want to grab coffee with me in a few hours. Her reply? "Sorry, I don't drink coffee, but if you want to take me for tea, I'll meet ya."

I could practically see her coy smile through the screen like she knew she had me hooked. At that moment, I thought, *"This is it—the one."* She didn't just captivate me; she threw me knuckleballs, and I was more than ready to play.

After that first "tea" date, we started chatting online every night, and before long, those chats turned into more dates and countless hours spent together. We'd meet whenever we could, making the most of any free time just to be together. The more we talked, the more we discovered we had in common—not just the usual likes and dislikes but a shared resilience shaped by the challenges we had overcome in our lives.

In the quiet moments, she opened up about her worries for Tommy, how she felt like she was living with this constant, invisible weight, always wondering if he'd be okay. She also shared her concerns for Frankie, feeling that he was missing out on simply being a kid, caught up in the whirlwind of Tommy's doctor's visits and treatments. She felt he'd been forced to grow up too fast, taking on responsibilities no young boy should carry. It weighed on her, knowing that while she focused on keeping Tommy safe, Frankie was quietly sacrificing pieces of his own childhood along the way.

The pain in her eyes was unmistakable, yet somehow, it only made her beauty more striking—like she carried a light through her struggles. I told her that, as hard as it was, some things were beyond anyone's control. What mattered was the life she was building with her boys, the joy she could choose to create with them now, rather than letting fear take up precious time.

From then on, our connection felt even deeper, grounded in something real and steady—an understanding that life was fleeting, and if we could laugh and find happiness together, even in the small moments, we had to make it count.

Dating Lisa did have its own unique quirks early on. The owner of the salon, a no-nonsense type with a soft spot, gave her the keys and offered her Sundays to work solo, letting her keep every penny she made. He understood what she was going through and wanted to help her get by with no strings attached.

So, every Sunday morning, rain or shine, a line of men would start to form outside that little storefront salon before she even turned on the lights. It was the sort of place that hadn't changed in years, complete with the cool people's posters on the wall, jars of combs soaking in that mysterious blue liquid, and a new odor in the air—a mix of strong men's cologne blending with the chemical punch of hair dye and perms. It seemed like all these men were boxing out all of Lisa's women clients!

These guys came in, looking like they'd stepped out of a casting call, each one convinced he was her biggest fan and some even bearing gifts—boxes of chocolates, flowers, and, strangely enough, shoes. Who brings shoes to a hair appointment? But sure enough, there they were, hoping a pair of stilettos might win her heart. I knew exactly what the fuck they wanted—they weren't just there for a trim and a shave.

But Lisa, in her own gracious way, handled them all like a pro, giving each one exactly what he paid for—no more, no less. She kept things all business, all charm and poise, letting each admirer think he had a shot while still keeping the boundary clear. She had a way of disarming their bullshit with a smile and a quick flick of her scissors, the kind of class that made me laugh and fall for her even more.

One of these admirers, a bit too full of himself, crossed the line. This guy was a good-looking and confident bastard who owned a business right on the same strip. Every Sunday, like clockwork, he'd come in for a trim, all swagger and charm, thinking he had an exclusive hold on her attention. Lisa, being careful when she worked alone, always kept the salon door locked, only opening it for her clients.

One particular Sunday, he was her last appointment. She unlocked the door to let him in, leaving the key in the lock for convenience, and told him to settle into the chair while she tidied up a few things in the back room. That's when he decided to make his move. Instead of sitting down, he walked up to the front door, turned the lock, and then quietly followed her to the back. Before she knew it, he was right behind her, his hands sliding around her waist, turning her to face him.

Lisa, usually quick on her feet, felt this shock of fear. As a stylist, she'd had her fair share of over-eager Italian Stallion crushes, but this was something else. She knew she had to act fast. Flashing him a polite but quivering smile, she said, "Listen, you seem like a nice guy, but two things you need to know: I'm just not attracted to you, and I've got a long-time boyfriend."

Her tone was confident, almost friendly, and it threw him off just enough. His boldness cracked visibly, and he blinked like a crazy person, looking at her with a surprise that came from rarely being turned down. Then, he stepped back, muttering something about getting back to his "usual trim."

Lisa, cool as a cucumber, kept her focus, guiding him back to the chair and silently looking up to God. She'd managed him without letting a flicker of fear show on her face, and by the time he left, he looked like a man thoroughly put in his place.

Lisa made the mistake of telling me the whole story. I made sure she was okay, but I was not.

The next Sunday, I found myself parked outside the salon, getting more and more agitated as I watched everyone walking to Mass. As I sat in my car, I felt a storm brewing—not in the sky, but in me. I was pissed that this guy thought he could take advantage of Lisa.

Finally, the bastard pulled up, stepping out with that same cocky swagger that only annoyed me more. He gave a quick look around, clearly unaware I was sitting right there, then strolled toward the salon.

I took a breath and waited, forcing myself to stay in the car a few minutes longer. But patience isn't exactly my strong suit, and before I knew it, my hand was on my car door handle. Then, I clicked my car alarm, letting it beep obnoxiously loud, and headed toward the salon.

I knocked, and Lisa, with a slightly confused, concerned look on her face, opened the door and let me in. I didn't say much, just gave her a nod, and parked myself in the station right next to where she was cutting his hair. I could feel him figuring out who I was, tossing me a glance, but he quickly went back to talking to Lisa, launching into a long, self-important monologue about his new cars and recent "business" trips to Europe. I sat there, watching him drone on, my jaw clenched as I replayed the nerve he'd shown last week.

That's when I noticed the Snapple bottle on the counter. Every time this guy opened his mouth, I slammed it on the stand. He'd be mid-sentence, talking about his BMW or some villa he stayed at, and then—SLAM!—I'd slam the bottle down. He'd flinch, shoot me a look, but keep going.

Lisa looked at me, clearly getting stressed out, but after the third time, I didn't need to slam the bottle anymore. He got the picture. The rest of the haircut was done in strained silence, him sitting uncomfortably while Lisa finished up, barely lifting his eyes from his own lap.

When Lisa was done with his haircut, he tossed some cash on the counter with barely a glance, muttered a hasty "thanks," and made a beeline for the door, regretting he didn't come at a different time that morning. As I stood up, the Snapple bottle squeezed in my hand, Lisa shot me a look—half pleading, half exasperated—trying to convince me to let it go. But I was already in motion. There was no way this guy was walking away without knowing exactly who I was.

I stepped outside, catching him just as he reached his Beemer. He looked up, and the color drained from his face when he saw me standing there. I leaned in, close enough that he couldn't look anywhere else but right at me, and said, "Don't fuckin' think about stepping back in that salon or this bottle is going to be embedded in your face. Do we have an understanding?"

He gave a shaky nod. He managed to get out one word, "Yup," and practically dove into his car. I watched him leave, and it was priceless. From that Sunday on, Lisa had one less client—and I had the satisfaction of knowing he wouldn't be bothering her again.

You'd think having all these so-called knights in shining armor would be an issue, right? Not a chance. Her ex, though? Now *he* was something else entirely. This dude had delusions of grandeur, convinced somehow that he'd get her back. There wasn't a chance in hell that it was going to happen—even if I wasn't dating Lisa. Their relationship was over a long time ago, but Lisa stayed for a while when Tommy was diagnosed with leukemia.

But as our relationship deepened, he took a dark turn. He'd call up, sometimes for hours, ranting and raving, throwing around fucking threats, thinking he could shake us. And when he wasn't tying up the line, he'd send these subliminal messages through the kids after their weekend visits, telling them things like how he'd heard about some woman on Staten Island who got shot by her ex-husband just yesterday. He knew exactly what he was doing, trying to scare the shit out of Lisa.

All the time she was going through this shit, I knew I wanted to give her an engagement ring. I couldn't think of a better time than the fall. Sure, it was a tough season for her—Tommy had been diagnosed at that time of year, and it always left her feeling a little down. But I figured, why not turn that around? Show her that no matter how bad things seem, they don't get to define a whole season—or a whole life.

So, one day, I took Frankie and Tommy out to lunch—just the three of us. Lisa wasn't there, so I could talk to them privately. I asked them straight out if I could marry their mom. As soon as I got the words out, they looked at each other, then looked back at me, and smiled. No hesitation. That was all the approval I needed.

I got to work on a plan to make the proposal unforgettable. With Frankie and Tommy's help, we carved "Marry Me, Lisa" inside a heart on a tree in Clove Lakes Park in Staten Island. That park meant everything to us—so many hours of walking, talking, and just being together there. The tree I picked was right by a little waterfall, tucked away in the woods. Perfect.

That Saturday morning, it was one of those crisp, sunny, fall days. I went to the park early in the morning and laid a trail of red rose petals from the road to the tree. Then I picked Lisa up from her shop after work and told her I wanted to take a walk in the park. She loved a good walk, so of course, she said yes.

As we strolled through the park, I steered her toward the road where I'd started the petals. She noticed them right away. "Look at this," she said, "Rose petals? Wonder why they are here." I played it cool and said, "Let's follow 'em and find out. Looks like they lead somewhere."

We walked along the path, her curiosity building, until we reached the tree. I had to nudge her a little. "What's that on the tree?" I asked while I was shaking inside.

She saw the carving, and the second she realized what it said, her eyes filled with tears. She couldn't even stand, she was so overwhelmed. I had to sit her down on a big boulder right next to the tree. And there, with the sound of the waterfall in the background, I asked her to marry me and put the ring on her finger.

The joy wasn't all smooth sailing, though—it had its share of bumps. A couple of months later, on a bitterly cold winter morning, Lisa went outside to warm up the car so the boys could get in nice and toasty before school. But when she walked over, she noticed something off—the windows were blacked out like they were tinted. She was puzzled for a second, but then it hit her: the whole car had been torched from the inside. She called me at work, and I could hear it in her voice right away. She asked me to get to the apartment as fast as I could; she'd already called 9-1-1, and the police and fire marshal were on their way because the car had been set on fire overnight.

When I got there, the car was burnt to a crisp inside. The seats were charred, the windows were smoked up, and the plastic console and dashboard were melted. As coincidence would have it, the fire marshal on the scene was an old buddy of mine from the neighborhood. We hadn't seen each other in years, so there was this quick, mini-reunion. But he didn't skip a beat, getting right into the job. He told me it looked like arson; he said they'd found an accelerant poured all over the seats.

That's when it hit me: only one other person had a set of keys to that car. I looked at him, and I told him I had a fucking good idea who was behind this. He asked me for a name and address, saying he'd go interview the guy, but I held back. I knew that kind of move might just provoke him, and the last thing I wanted was to drag Lisa or the boys through more of this. The fire marshal got it right away, nodded, and said to give him a call if we ever changed our minds.

In the weeks that followed, when I shared the story with a few acquaintances, more than one of them offered to "handle it," if you know what I mean. But I didn't bite. That's not how you handle things as an adult. I'm not a kid, and I've learned that things like this have a way of working out over time. Besides, I wasn't about to stoop to his level. We were building something real, something he'd never touch—and that was enough for me.

In the end, things with her ex unfortunately had term limits. No matter how much we tried to keep him involved in the boys' lives, he decided to take a bow and exit stage left. Just like that, he was gone—physically, emotionally, financially. He took them off his health insurance, cutting ties in every sense of the word. That was when I knew it was time to step up and marry Lisa right then and there.

It wasn't as though marriage wasn't already on the horizon, but this moved things along. I wanted to make sure those boys were taken care of, especially Tommy, who had a pre-existing condition. Without immediate action, he'd be left uninsured and unprotected, and that wasn't something I could let happen.

So, we didn't waste another minute. I married Lisa down at City Hall the day before New Year's, just in time for the health insurance to kick in on January 1st!

I got the boys on my plan, and right then and there, we became a family in every way that mattered. What he couldn't see was that his attempts to shake us had only strengthened us. We were in it together, and nothing—not his absence, not his actions, not his words—was ever going to change that.

And just like that, we became an instant family! We immediately found a beautiful home in New Jersey and moved in—err, right after Lisa thoroughly vetted the school and its principal to make sure the system was a good fit for Frankie and Tommy. During our meeting, Lisa shared her concerns about transitioning the boys from a small parochial school to a larger public one. The principal listened with a smile and said, "Let's take a walk. As we pass the classrooms, imagine the students wearing uniforms. You won't notice the difference."

And he was right! It felt just like a private school, the kind we were accustomed to back in New York. He then took the time to introduce us to some teachers, parents, and even the school custodian. Everyone was so kind and welcoming—it almost didn't feel real. That meeting sealed the deal for us. Bordentown wasn't just a place to live; it was a place we knew we could call home.

Frankie and Tommy quickly made new friends, and Simba—our new puppy gifted to Tommy by a cancer foundation—absolutely loved the extra space the house provided. Seeing them so happy filled Lisa and me with pure joy.

Next, we quickly got the news that Lisa was pregnant just a couple of months after we were married... what can I say? I have powerful engines! The boys were over the moon with excitement. When Ryan came into our lives, he didn't just complete our family; he brought us even closer together. The boys adored him from the start, and their bond has only grown stronger over the years. Watching them interact, laugh, look out for each other, and just be brothers has been one of life's greatest joys for Lisa and me.

What was coming up in a few years for me was an enormous challenge for my family. They had already been through so much, and I knew they didn't deserve the added stress and burden that I was about to place on them. It was going to be incredibly tough for them, and to this day, I feel guilty, knowing they had to bear that weight.

Chapter 13

Real Estate, Shmeal Estate

In 2004, I decided to walk away from real estate—not because I wasn't good at it, but because I was too good. Selling houses on Staten Island back then was like running with a pack of wolves. Realtors would do anything for a commission—*anything*. The houses started popping up so close together that you could practically borrow sugar from your neighbor without even leaving your chair. Staten Island lost that magic it had when I was a kid. Back then, we had these big open spaces to run through, places where you could actually *breathe*. Now? Every inch was stuffed with a house, a car, and then another house crammed right behind it.

Real estate stories always have something fucking strange. This one deal, I was closing on a property for a client, and the seller insisted on a last-minute walkthrough. The tenant was all nervous about her landlord—there'd been some threats flying back and forth. To keep it from getting messy, I offered to help her move, so she wouldn't need to deal with the landlord herself. I told her, "Go hang at a friend's place or something; I'll handle giving the keys back for you." I knew this was going to be a tense one—and wouldn't you know it, it was.

It was like 95 degrees in July, and—of course—they turned the AC off on her. I was sweating through my shirt, gathering boxes, and someone knocked on the door. There she is—the seller—demanding an inspection *right now*. This had nothing to do with me. I was just trying to do everybody a favor. But you know what they say—no good deeds go unpunished.

I asked her if she could give me a few minutes to wrap things up, since the movers were about to show, and I didn't want to hold them up. Without even thinking, I was leaning against the doorframe—I might have been blocking her way a little. Well, she wasn't having it. She shoved my arm aside and barged right past me like she owned the place—oh, right, she *did* own the place.

Between the stress, the heat, and no AC, I was straight-up melting. So, I figured, what the hell—took off my soaked shirt to cool down a little. Next thing I know, she's screaming like a lunatic, whipping out her phone, and calling the cops! She started telling them I stripped down and tried to assault her. I'm standing there with my jaw on the floor, thinking, *"Are you kiddin' me?"*

One of the neighbors poked his head in and asked if I need a hand because everyone knew she was bat-shit crazy. I told him, "Nah, thanks, you're better off staying out this—you gotta live next door to her, not me."

When the cops showed up, they came in with their hands on their holsters, and there I was, sitting like a deer in headlights. I tried to explain who I was and what I was doing there, and I tried to be friendly. I put my hand on one of the officers' shoulders. Big mistake.

He spun around, gun out, yelling, "Sit the fuck down and don't touch me!" Yeah, not exactly how I pictured my day. I thought I'd be at the movies by now, kicking back and eating some popcorn like a fat bastard.

So, I explained the whole thing—how the tenant had a beef with the landlord, and I was just there playing the middleman. They told me to sit tight while they go interview the seller. Meanwhile, I called my cousin, who was a sergeant at the same precinct. I barely got through the story before he laughed so hard, he accidentally hung up on me! Oh yeah, real funny—except not so much for me at the moment.

A couple of minutes later, the cops came back in, right as my cousin called me back. When I told them who was on the line, their whole vibe changed. One of them snatched my phone and said, "Johnny Tripoli, you fuckin' asshole, is that you?"

Next thing I knew, they were ribbing each other back and forth like old drinking buddies. Then they started telling my cousin how the lady was off her rocker. She even tried showing them some old, faded bruise, claiming I gave it to her—but it looked more like bloodwork performed during the week.

After all the back-and-forth, they handed me my phone, laughing, and said, "Just leave the keys in the apartment." And, of course, they threw in, "Next time, maybe don't touch the cops," chuckling as they walked out. That was it—I was free to go with the "official verdict" being what we all know: sanity beats crazy every time.

Staten Island really is its own little universe. You'd see families driving around in these massive SUVs at noon like it's Sunday every day. And I'm thinking, *"Does anybody even work out here? And how the hell are they affording these gas guzzlers?"* Half the time, the trucks were bigger than the houses they were squeezed in front of, crammed into these tiny driveways with an inch of clearance on each side.

And don't even get me started on the so-called "gold-plated" expectations. People thought their houses were worth a fortune just because they swapped out a couple of fixtures. You'd see listings bragging about "luxury upgrades," and it's a faucet that's just a little shinier than the last one! Between the cutthroat agents, the sky-high prices, and all the "luxury" nonsense, I figured my sanity—and my morals—would be better off somewhere else... or so I thought.

As much as real estate wasn't exactly my thing, it ended up being a blessing in disguise for me and Lisa. Sure, the job drove me nuts sometimes, but it gave me great flexibility. That was something you don't get with most nine-to-fives. It let us grab time together in ways that other couples only dream about.

Back then, if I wasn't running around the Island with showings or listings, we'd sneak off for a quick lunch. Sometimes we'd hop in the car and take drives, cutting through Staten Island's winding roads and talking nonstop. Other times, we'd stroll along the boardwalk with Brooklyn and the Verrazzano Bridge right there in the background. A lot of it was spur-of-the-moment, but those little escapes gave her a break from the everyday stress—and, honestly, they kept me grounded too.

Lisa and I got together a bit later in life, but honestly, it feels like we've packed a lifetime into the years we've spent together. It's funny—most people think of relationships as measured by time, by anniversaries, by the years that stack up. But with us, every moment has had a kind of richness to it, a depth that's hard to put into words. How can I not put it into words if I'm writing a book? Well, here it goes... Geez!

When you meet someone later on, after you've had your share of ups and downs, it's like you already know what's worth holding onto. We'd both lived enough life to not waste time on the nonsense. From the start, it was like we were on the same page—no fussing over the small stuff, just diving into the things that make a relationship feel... timeless.

The days and years with Lisa have been packed with memories like we're living two lifetimes in one. Every moment we've had—whether it's a late-night chat, a quiet lunch, or a walk hand-in-hand through Staten Island or Jersey—feels bigger than anything I ever imagined. And that's the magic of it, isn't it?

Chapter 14

Fresh Start in Ground Zero's Shadow

I was done with real estate—done chasing those inconsistent commissions and always wondering if I'd sell enough to keep some cash in my pocket. I had a family now, and I needed something steady, something real.

So, I started putting the word out, asking around, dropping hints to friends: "If you hear about somethin' solid, lemme know." All I needed was a shot. I knew if someone gave me a chance, I'd show them what I was made of.

One day, someone from this networking group I belonged to suggested I call his buddy who got involved with a new company in downtown Manhattan. They were looking for a salesperson. The gig seemed promising: rebuilding downtown after 9/11, focusing on emergency preparedness and an engineering wing.

A qualified engineer was required for both existing and new construction projects. It had legs, as they say, rebuilding wasn't going to happen overnight, and if this panned out, it meant job security.

I made the call, and a few days later, I found myself walking into their office—a big space just a block away from Ground Zero. The city was all-in on bringing life back to the area, throwing grants at companies like theirs to set up shop there. The commute wasn't too bad either, just a train ride from Jersey.

The company was called Domestic Infrastructure Development. There were a few owners running around the place, but the two I met with couldn't have been more opposite.

First up was Charles Desiderio. This guy looked like he walked straight out of a Wall Street magazine cover—polished, sharp suit and tie, and a mustache that looked like it hadn't left the '80s. He leaned back against the front of his desk while he talked casually, making sure he put me at ease. And his voice was that raspy, college-boy, "I spend my weekends on the Upper East Side" kind of tone. We chatted for about 45 minutes, and I got to hand it to him—the guy made sense.

Then there was Jack Alessio—big guy, rough around the edges, no suit, no tie, and definitely not throwing around any fancy words. He had that no-nonsense vibe I grew up seeing, the kind of guy who doesn't sugarcoat anything. I figured college wasn't part of his backstory, and I wasn't wrong. Jack didn't waste a second. As soon as Charles wrapped up, he stepped in and laid it all out in five minutes flat—salary, benefits, start date. "You're good with it? Be here Monday," he said.

Before I even got a chance to respond, he shoved a list of clients in my hand and told me I'd be signed up for an emergency preparedness course. No chitchat, no fluff—just straight to business.

These two couldn't have been more opposite, but somehow it worked. They had a vision and something about it drew me in. After talking it over with Lisa, I said yes. Looking back, that moment felt like a lifeline, a fresh start, right there in the shadow of where the towers once stood. And for the first time in a long while, it felt like I was about to be part of something bigger than myself.

I hit the ground fucking running when I started there. Sure, I had a bit of luck on my side, but most of it was me putting my big boy pants on. I brought in ideas that worked—training courses, lunch-and-learn seminars, and just hammering the phones, calling the right people. Slowly but surely, I found my rhythm. The engineering side of the business seemed to click better for me, so I doubled down on it. Within months, I was making a name for myself in the industry.

But success doesn't come without strings. After a while, Jack Alessio started asking more personal questions. At first, I didn't think much of it—it was him taking an interest. Now? I see it plain as day, that's when he started grooming me. Guys like Jack have a radar for sniffing out vulnerabilities. They scope out the wounded ducks and figure out where they can hook you. He saw I'd just married into an instant family, had no safety net, and needed steady money and health insurance. So, he started feeding me promises... big ones. Money that made my head spin.

And for a while, I fell for it. I was bringing in so much business, the company's growing pains started hitting me right where it hurt—my paycheck. Commission checks weren't showing up in my account anymore. I had to chase them down, practically begging for the money I earned.

Three years of busting my ass, putting my family on the back burner for this job, and I'd finally had it. The last straw came when I sat down with Charles to talk about the $34,000 they owed me. He gave me that fake, surprised look like he didn't know it was that much. "Let me talk to Jack," he said. "We'll get you a third now and settle the rest next month."

And then I heard it—Jack's voice, booming from the next room: "No fuckin' salesman is gonna be makin' more money than me!"

Did I need a freakin' piano to fall on my head at that point? Geez! All the promises, all the big talk—it was bullshit. Right then, something clicked. I knew my time there was done. Life was about to change in ways I couldn't have imagined, and I was nowhere near ready for it.

Chapter 15

From the Pot to the Frying Pan

Looking back, with a bit of self-taught experience under my belt, I figured it was time to aim higher and start interviewing at companies in the same industry. That's when I bumped into Terence O'Leary at a tradeshow in Manhattan. We started chatting and I opened up about my situation. He was all ears.

Terence ran a business called Engineering Marvels, pretty close to what I was doing, and he threw out the idea of me jumping ship to help him run the place. I made what I now realize was a hasty decision and signed a big contract in no time. It felt right back then, and my clients were ready to follow me, and they did.

Early on, I started having lunch regularly with John Rizzo, Engineering Marvel's CFO. Rizzo came off as a sharp guy, the kind who had his shit together, and these lunches quickly became a daily thing. Over time, Rizzo began venting about Terence. He didn't hold back, describing him as someone who wasn't quite what he seemed from the outside. Rizzo's dissatisfaction was evident, but I just listened, taking mental notes. I wasn't about to judge until I saw things with my own eyes.

It didn't take long for Rizzo's words to hit home. My second paycheck from Terence dropped into my bank account, and it was half of what I was owed. I thought I was seeing things, so I marched right into his office, hoping it was some kind of clerical mistake. Nah.

Terence looked at me all smug and said, "It's not a mistake. I can't afford to pay what's in your contract. We need to renegotiate." Renegotiate? Without me? He'd already decided what I was worth and made his move. It's like trying to have sex by yourself—only one person's going to get any satisfaction outta that.

That was it for me. I snapped. Right there in his office, I slammed my laptop shut, stuffed it in my briefcase, and gave him a piece of my mind. "How the fuck you gonna pull this shit on a man with a family and a mortgage?!" I told him I was done and stormed out.

But as the elevator doors closed behind me, the reality of what I'd just done started hitting me. Quit? Without a backup plan? How the hell could I be so reckless? I have responsibilities—Lisa and the boys depended on me. And, as usual, I hadn't even talked this through with her. My rage got the best of me, and now here I was, unemployed and unprepared, spiraling straight into the land of fuckville.

Down in the lobby, I paced like a madman, trying to figure out a plan from the mess I just made. And then, out of nowhere, John Rizzo steps off the elevator. He comes up to me and says, "I'm gonna quit too... Why don't we start our own business? Let's grab some food and talk about it."

At lunch, I was honest with him. "John, I'm not in any financial position to fund a payroll or even pay myself. We also gotta make sure we got enough engineers for these projects." But Rizzo started talking about factoring receivables, something I'd worked with back in my garment industry days. The more he went on, the more it started making sense. Against my better judgment, or just out of desperation, I decided to take the leap.

We launched Engineering Consultants of Manhattan, a name Rizzo cooked up that I absolutely hated, but hey, there were bigger fish to fry like making money and getting health insurance. Clients followed me like they always did, and we scored a solid gig with a client who had a 27-story, new construction building. We put an engineer on the job full-time, and the invoices started rolling out. The factoring company loved it. For a minute, it looked like this gamble might actually pay off.

And then, out of nowhere, the world flipped on its head. The stock market crashed. That big client was Lehman Brothers. They went belly up overnight, leaving us holding the bag on $60,000 in invoices that weren't ever going to get paid. The high-risk, high-reward dream I jumped into so blindly had us behind the 8-ball from the start.

Our luck began to change though, and I had a steady stream of high-end clients starting to sign contracts. These included property management companies overseeing some of the world's most exclusive properties overlooking Central Park, as well as general contractors and participants in training classes throughout the city.

Engineers weren't exactly growing on trees. But we were small enough, so I managed to scrounge up enough talent to keep the wheels turning. Every project we had going on, we were covered—barely, but we were covered. Now, don't get me wrong, in the back of my head, I knew there'd come a day when there weren't going to be enough of them to go around. But I didn't sit around worrying about it. I shoved that thought into the "stuff to freak out about later" pile and kept moving. One fire at a time, you know?

In the meantime, riding the subway through Manhattan, stepping out from underground, seeing the city open up in front of me was something else. Everywhere I looked—every corner, every block—it hit me. Many of those buildings and construction sites weren't just random spots on a map. Those were my jobs, the stuff I brought in, and the deals I made. It gave me this feeling like I made it, and I was proud of how far I'd come... even if it was just for what seemed like a fleeting moment.

Chapter 16

Trouble in Paradise

As the business grew, so did Rizzo's ego and arrogance. I had clients and staff calling me, saying they only wanted to deal with me because, plain and simple, he was a piece of shit. The guy worked the system like an expert. He had everyone coming to me because I was the nice guy and, frankly, because nobody could stand him. I'm a people person, so I didn't mind picking up the slack, but after a while, I started noticing how his attitude was shifting. He was getting more difficult to work with, and I could feel the tension building. I didn't want that to screw up the relationships I'd worked so hard to build.

Like I said before, I didn't know squat about the financial side of things, so I left that in his hands and, honestly, that was a decision I'd come to regret big time. He'd show me the ledgers, and everything looked legit. Clean, neat—nothing that would make you think twice.

But the problem was, we were always coming up short, always scrambling to stay liquid. I'd ask him what was going on, and he'd hit me with some excuse. "Oh, I underpaid an engineer here," or "I miscalculated what we owed the state over there." At first, it sounded believable enough, like he just made a mistake or two. But after a while, I started getting that gut feeling, ya know? Something wasn't adding up. Turns out, the bastard was cooking the books the whole time, pulling some shady moves behind the scenes, and I was too busy focusing on the other fires to catch it.

When I'd press him on my concerns, he'd flip the script every time and start yelling things like, "What are we, a bank?" Back then, I didn't even know what gaslighting was, but now I'm an expert! Honestly, I can't believe I kept my cool with this prick for as long as I did. He'd make me feel like I was the one overreacting, like I was the crazy one for asking questions. Deep down, I knew I should've walked away from his nonsense, but I was stuck in the middle, trying to keep everything afloat. I had bills to pay, health insurance that had to stay active, and don't get me started on the life insurance I had through the company.

His shit started to weigh on me so heavily, it was like I couldn't breathe. It was messing with my head, affecting everything—my whole demeanor was starting to change. I wasn't the same guy anymore. I was getting drained just trying to keep everything together while he kept taking me for a ride.

I felt trapped—like I was stuck in the middle, juggling the business, trying to drum up more work, constantly playing defense, and trying to protect everyone from Rizzo's crap. The guy had this slick way of shielding himself from the financial mess, always finding some excuse, some way to make it look like it wasn't his fault. But deep down, I knew the truth was catching up with him—and with me, too. It was like an avalanche, all this pressure crushing me, and I couldn't outrun it. The weight of it all was unbearable. But I kept pushing, thinking I could fix it and save what I'd built. I had to make sure it wasn't all for nothing. Even though every day felt like one more step closer to my breaking point, I kept telling myself I could turn it around.

Chapter 17

The Cancer Chronicles

All the pressure from the business was piling up, and then life decided to kick me in the balls—I got cancer. One morning, I dragged myself out of bed, jumped in the shower, and looked in the mirror, half-hoping to see Brad Pitt staring back. Instead, I saw this big lump at the base of my neck. Never noticed it before, and it was way too large to ignore. I showed Lisa, and we wasted no time getting a doctor's appointment that day.

The doc didn't seem too freaked out at first, saying it might just be a lipoma, but she couldn't explain why it showed up out of nowhere. She sent me for an ultrasound, and wouldn't you know it, that turned into a biopsy. This shit started to get real. It was Thanksgiving week—the same friggin' time of year Tommy was diagnosed with leukemia. Talk about déjà vu from a bad dream.

Lisa and I were at the supermarket, grabbing stuff to cook for Thanksgiving, trying to pretend things were normal—when I got the call. The doctor wanted to see me ASAP. I didn't need a crystal ball to figure it out—they don't call you in for face-to-face chats to tell you good news. That's the kind of call that makes your stomach drop, and mine hit the fucking floor.

Turns out, the lump was nothing, but they found nodules on my thyroid that were cancerous. And just my luck—the doctor told me the surgery to remove it wasn't going to be a walk in the park. My neck didn't have enough room because I was too muscular. Yeah, not exactly the kind of compliment you want to hear when someone's about to cut you open!

This couldn't have come at a worse time. I already had the weight of the business and Rizzo's bullshit dragging me down, and now I had to put everything on hold to deal with this crap. It felt like I was stuck at the bottom of Johnny-on-the-Pony, and everybody and their mother were piling on and crushing me.

Here's one of the smartest moves I thought I made during all of this—I called Rizzo and told him the news. Then I told him to take my name off the business and change the company name. I would remain running operations as an employee when I got back. I didn't want Lisa tied to this schmuck if I kicked the bucket. It was the right call, but it wasn't enough to shield me from the bullshit he was going to pull in the months I was recovering.

While all this shit was going on, an architect buddy of mine introduced me to Vincent, a guy in a similar line of work to us. He had a load of engineering projects but didn't have the time to vet the right staff for each one. That's where we stepped in.

Before all the hospital drama kicked off, I set up a meeting. I introduced Vincent to Rizzo and told them to hash it out while I focused on planning for my surgery and recovery.

Rizzo told me it wasn't going anywhere with Vincent, which, honestly, isn't unusual in business. Sometimes you talk to people, pick their brains, and it just doesn't click. So, I didn't think much of it at the time. But here's the thing—Vincent's name is going to pop up again soon.

Fast forward to the surgery and the health insurance clusterfuck I've already laid out earlier in the book. The surgery finally happened, and—surprise, surprise— there were complications, just like the surgeon warned me about. Not only did they have a hell of a time ripping out the thyroid, but the cancer had spread. They ended up not only taking out the thyroid but also two of my parathyroids (whatever the hell those are) and a bunch of lymph nodes for good measure. Now between this and the health insurance issues, I'm a walking mess.

To top it off, the surgeon had to fiddle around near my voice box, leaving me with a drain sticking out of my neck. It looked like they were siphoning gasoline from my tank. What was supposed to be a quick 45-minute in-and-out job turned into a six-hour marathon.

I was stuck in the hospital for a few days recovering, and the whole time I'm sitting there thinking, "*Look at all these poor sick people.*" Meanwhile, it hits me—I'm one of them! Can you believe that? Me, in the same boat as everyone else.

When the doctor finally came in to check on me, I was ready. I had my questions written down on a piece of paper. The big one at the top was, "*When will I get my voice back?*" And what does this arrogant prick say?

"I just saved your life, and you're worried about your voice?" Seriously, who the hell does this guy think he was? Talk about no bedside manners. Like, thanks for saving me and all, but try not to act like a total asshole while you're at it.

The months that followed were a blur of radiation treatments, no voice, and feeling like total crap. I was sluggish, worn out, and barely functioning. And that's when Rizzo saw his opening.

"Don't worry about the business," he said, all concerned. "I'll handle it. I'll do double duty—operations and finances." Yeah, right.

He told me to just stay home, send out any contracts to clients, and text anyone trying to call me, telling them to reach out to him instead because I couldn't speak on the phone yet. At the time, I was too beat up to argue. It sounded like he was stepping up, but really, it was the perfect setup for him to run the whole show without me watching.

Chapter 18

The Patient is Running the Asylum

Now that I was out of commission, Rizzo started cutting corners left and right. The company's team was supposed to consist of qualified engineers who'd sign off on permits and ensure projects were done by the book. That was the whole point: keeping everything legit. But Rizzo saw how sloppy the city's system was and smelled an opportunity.

Here's how it worked: the city handed you the actual permit, which the engineer would take to a notary, sign it, and return it to the Department of Buildings. Once that was done, the project could move forward. Simple, right? Too simple. It took me a while, but I began to hear whispers and see inconsistencies in Rizzo's new business practices and how he tried to play the system.

He figured, why pay a real engineer's salary when he could pay guys who weren't qualified half as much to sign off on permits? He even created fake certificates to make them look legit. And if that weren't enough, he'd have these stand-ins forge the signatures of real engineers with a shady notary backing them up. The dumb-dumb notary would risk his livelihood and look the other way for pennies. Unreal!

The fucking guy turned the operation into a complete scam while I was sidelined. Soon he riddled the projects with phony engineers. I always had very little faith in him, but I thought I was clear of the nonsense, not realizing the scope of the fraud he was committing. I insulated myself from the operations and just made sales calls from home as an employee now. In the meantime, he was running wild in the city, cutting every corner he could find, and dragging the business, and my name, into his mess.

Between the health insurance debacle, unraveling the fraud of bogus engineers on projects, and the rollercoaster paychecks, the anvil finally hit me on the head: I was out. Done. I had to leave a ton of money on the table that was owed to me. Who knows what the actual amount really was—anywhere from a half million to a million dollars! But I knew who I was as a person, and this wasn't me. I was better than this. This left me in a different bind—no job, no clear game plan, and, to top it off, mounting pressure to keep my family's healthcare intact. Fuck! I can't believe that I got sucked up in this business deal and didn't have a better handle on it.

So, I called Rizzo and pussied out with a cockamamy excuse that the whole thing wasn't working out. I ended the convo with something like, "If you need me to do you a favor and make a call here or there, I'd try and help you out."

I was sidestepping the truth about the crime machine he'd built—a machine powered by my hard work and the trust of clients I'd cultivated. I wanted to lay it all out for him, to confront him with the sleaze-bag vibes I felt every time I had to deal with him, but instead, I let him off easy and just walked away from it all. I was trying to untangle myself from something rotten, even if it meant leaving behind all that cash. I was so fucking stupid—I should have just told him the truth and made a clean break from this schmuck!

And then, with no other choice, I picked up the phone and started working my connections. It didn't take long to find a lead. A buddy in the same line of work was thrilled to hear I was untethered, though I'm sure his excitement had more to do with the million-dollar signed contracts I was ready to bring over before I even clocked in.

We met, and over coffee, I gave him the highlights of my fallout with Rizzo, laying it out straight. I needed stability for my family, and I needed it fast. He told me to hang tight and give him a couple of weeks to sort things out. The deal we made with the salary and healthcare sounded great, so I offered to get my customers to sign on with him.

I got proactive. I reached out to my clients, changed the contracts with the new company, got both parties signed, and waited. Weeks turned into months, and the silence on his end started to feel like I was being ghosted by some girl back in high school. I kept following up, hopeful for a start date. Then, out of the blue, I got a text to meet him at the Freedom Tower downtown.

The moment I walked into that meeting, I could feel it in the air that it wasn't going to be good news. Sure enough, he laid it out: "Rich, I can't bring you on right now. Things have slowed down; we can't justify the extra payroll."

I just stared at him, trying to process what he just said. Finally, I got in his face and said, "But you were fine taking the business I brought you."

He didn't have an answer, and as I left, the reality hit me like a freight train. The noose was tightening. By the time I was halfway home, it felt like the world was closing in on me, pressing tighter every second. There wasn't even enough room in the train car to hold the weight of it all, let alone the entire world that seemed determined to crush me.

Chapter 19

This Shit is Getting Real

Once again, here I am, out on the street, pounding the pavement with my resume in one hand and a client list in the other. I'm trying to revive the business I worked so hard to build. But here's the catch: I still need someone backing the venture financially, an entity to stand behind my efforts.

I've heard about a few events happening in Manhattan that could offer some solid networking opportunities. In the meantime, Rizzo—yeah, again—calls me up for a couple of cell numbers he needs and asks what I'm up to. I tell him I'm going to various events in the next week or so.

For some reason, I told him I was going to the big event at the Jacob Javits Center the following week. Why am I still entertaining this clown? But, whatever, this event always attracts the right crowd, and I figured I could at least create some waves about my new plans.

It was like I could see his smug face through the phone, and he oozes the words, "Maybe I'll see ya there."

As I'm riding the train to the Javits that day, something doesn't sit right with me. At first, I brush it off as pre-event jitters, the weight of trying to find stability in life. But as usual, I'm wrong. When I finally get to the registration table, I hand over my info, and the woman pulls up my nametag with all my old info on it. I rolled my eyes because I thought they just recycled my details from the previous year.

What I didn't realize was that this was just another one of Rizzo's little games. See, he was pissed I bailed, and now he's trying to rope me back into his web of lies. Turns out, he'd told the registration desk to slap his company name on my nametag. Well, instead of changing it, I just flipped it over and printed my own name and info on the blank side.

Here's the fucked up part—I don't know if it was at the last minute, but Rizzo actually rented a booth, highlighting his company's services. As I strolled through the event, I spotted about five guys behind a booth who looked like they had just stepped out of a Brooklyn social club. None of them looked familiar, and frankly, I had no idea who they were. The whole thing felt surreal because I looked up at the banner and it was Rizzo's company.

Then he came up behind me, all smiles, and said, "Go take a photo with all our guys." I stand there, confused. Why the hell would I take a picture with these delinquents? I'm not even with the company anymore.

Now I'm a mess and immediately begin to sweat. I had no idea what he was up to, but in hindsight, I figured it out. If he ever gets caught, he's planning to use that photo as "proof" that I was involved in his little scam. Maybe he thought it'd help him dodge some of the heat. Jesus, how does this guy even sleep at night? The thought of all the schemes and lies—it's exhausting.

So, I just shook my head, forgot about walking the rest of the place, and made my way out the front door because I didn't understand what just went on. By the time I left, I was in full panic-attack mode and sat on a park bench down the block from the event, confused at what had just happened. Do you see how smooth and calculating he can be? I'll be shedding light on this soon enough.

A few weeks after the big event at the Javits Center, I found myself walking down Central Park South on my way to an important meeting with a company I was counting on for financial backing. The city had that late-morning buzz, yellow cabs flying by, tourists tripping over themselves, and the occasional homeless person laying on cardboard. I was in my own head, prepping for the pitch, when I heard someone shout my name from across the avenue.

It was a buildings inspector I knew—a straight shooter, one of the rare ones in the city who didn't make you feel like every conversation was going to be a shake down. He hustled across the street, waving me down, and it was clear from his face this wasn't just a friendly stop-and-chat.

"I was gonna call you," he said, catching his breath. "There's a problem with one of your permits."

I felt the hair on my arms go up. Rizzo. Of course. Even though I'd washed my hands of that guy months ago, his name still had a way of sticking to me.

"I'm not involved with that company anymore," I told him, showing that I was detached from the company. "Couldn't take the guy's bullshit any longer."

"Well," the inspector said, lowering his voice, "then you're lucky, because there's a signature on a permit dated last week, and the guy who supposedly signed it has been dead for six months."

"What?" I said, while I felt like peeing in my pants.

"They're opening an investigation and, just warning you, it's probably gonna get ugly."

I nodded, pretending I was more relieved than surprised. "Yeah, that sucks. I knew Rizzo's games were gonna catch up to him eventually. Thank God I'm out of it."

The inspector gave me a look like he was trying to decide if I was telling the truth. After a quick goodbye, I kept moving, but the knot in my stomach only got worse. And it wasn't from the hotdog I grabbed from a cart at Columbus Circle.

I pulled out my phone and called Rizzo. No pleasantries, just straight to the point: I told him what the inspector said.

He let out this dismissive laugh, his usual mix of arrogance and denial, and said, "It's probably just old paperwork. Everything's legit with the new permits. And anyway, you're out, so what do you care?"

But in my mind, I was saying to myself: "You care because you walked away, knowing Rizzo was pulling shady shit. You looked the other way one too many times, and now the hens are coming home to roost."

I hung up the phone, half-believing his story. The other half was screaming that I should've gone to the right people a long time ago, spilled my guts, and cleaned my slate. But I also knew this much: I wasn't involved. If Rizzo's house of cards was about to collapse, I wouldn't be standing under it. At least, that's what I told myself as I tucked my phone away and tried to refocus on the meeting ahead.

A few weeks down the line, I got a call from some guy, claiming to be a potential client, looking for a proposal. Right off the bat, something about him just didn't sit right. I told him, "Listen, I'm not with the company anymore," but I stayed on the line because the whole thing felt... off. He gave me some generic name for the company he was supposedly with, but I knew most of the players in the city and that company didn't ring a bell. When I asked about the location of the project, he danced around the question like he was Fred Astaire.

Instead, he just kept hammering home that he needed someone to sign off on a permit for the job. Usually, these people are pretty friendly on the phone because they are in a bind. They can't start the project unless all the paperwork is submitted. This guy was neither friendly nor forthcoming with the info. He was like, "Don't worry about the particulars. I'll just send you the permit—have your guy sign it, and I'll send you the cash just for a signature."

It was screwy, plain and simple. So, I rattled off a couple of names of friendly competitors who could handle whatever nonsense this guy was peddling. I figured, let him be their problem. Turns out, this wasn't just some random dickhead call. It was the first thread unraveling, as it was the beginning of an investigation by the district attorney's office.

It wasn't hard for them to put two and two together after seeing a dead guy signing permits—and this call was part of a secret probe into the company. Once they started pulling on that thread, the whole operation began to come apart at the seams.

A little time went by, and I got a call from an architect I used to work with. He was a sharp guy who always had something brewing. This time, he wanted me to meet him and a friend of his, a guy who had a large Manhattan portfolio of properties—the kind that needed my expertise.

We were trying to figure out a good place to chat, so he suggested we meet at a restaurant in the West Village. A few months back, we'd talked about me going out on my own, and he knew I'd been having issues with my old partner. His friend was in a bind, needing eight engineers right away to get his projects moving. It sounded like the perfect chance to jumpstart my business and leave all the Rizzo mess behind.

So, I agreed to the meeting. Starting fresh, taking on something big—it all seemed promising. What I didn't know was how fucked-up things were about to get.

It was one of those late-autumn mornings where the city air smelled like a mix of roasted chestnuts from the street vendors and that feeling of the cold going right through your bones. The West Village was alive, as always—tree-lined streets with the leaves covering the sidewalk. The diner was on the corner, a throwback place that was all chrome on the outside and neon inside. When I entered, the warm air immediately hit me along with the smell of bacon and stale coffee.

I got there early; I've always been told that if you're on time, you're late. The place was humming with the usual crowd: a few students hunched over laptops, some construction workers being vulgar, and servers calling out orders with no regard for the morning hour. The warmth inside was a welcome contrast to the chill outside, but I noticed right away something was off. The two guys I was meeting were already there, seated at a booth with a motorcycle helmet that was plunked right in the center of the table. The helmet looked completely out of character for the two of them. They certainly weren't the motorcycle types.

Now, I was raised to know better than to leave a hat on a table because it was bad luck or just bad manners, depending on who you ask—but a helmet? I wasn't sure if that counted. Still, I let it go. The architect introduced me to his friend, a property owner with a portfolio of Manhattan buildings that had a problem with eight stalled projects, all waiting on engineers to get them moving.

The architect was the type of guy who usually cracked a joke or busted my chops. That day, his vibe was all business, which wasn't like him. The property owner, on the other hand, was a bit green when it came to the technical side of things. That didn't surprise me because most of these owners delegate the nuts and bolts to their project managers.

So, I walked him through the process, explaining how engineers sign off on permits and oversee the work. He nodded along, eager to keep the conversation moving toward one thing: could I deliver him eight engineers, right now, to get these projects rolling? Time, as they all put it, was money.

I was honest. "Look, I've got two qualified guys I can count on right now. The other six are gonna take some time to staff up. I'm not gonna cut corners."

The architect raised an eyebrow. "Can't you just get anyone to sign the permits, like you did with Rizzo?"

That hit a nerve. I leaned back with surprise and said, "You know I don't work that way. My ex-partner might've, but I like being able to sleep at night." I made the message clear that I wasn't going down that road again, no matter how much money was on the table.

Breakfast arrived—pancakes, eggs, and coffee—and that friggin' helmet stayed right where it was, right smack in the middle of the table. I tried to lighten the mood, joking, "You know, my mother would lose her mind if she saw a helmet on the table."

The property owner chuckled. "There's more room here than on the chairs," he said, brushing it off. I didn't care. I was already thinking ahead to the coordination of these jobs, the timelines, and the potential this deal could have for getting me back on my feet.

We wrapped up with an agreement that I'd send over a proposal: a timeline for the projects, cost breakdowns, and the terms for how we'd partner up. As we finished, I figured we'd all leave together, but the architect turned to me and said, "Me and him have some other business to discuss. You're good to go." The way he said it didn't sit right, but I let it slide. Sometimes things are just awkward, and I have other things to focus on.

The pace of this story picks up fast. It started with a call from a New York City detective from the DA's office. He introduced himself and told me he needed to meet me for an interview... today. I shivered at the thought of this. I'd already made it home for the day and tried to push it to the next day, but he wasn't budging.

"I can come to your house to make it easy," he said, "or we can meet someplace in between." The last thing I wanted was Lisa worrying about this mess, so I agreed to meet him at a rest stop on the Jersey Turnpike. Not exactly the most dignified spot, but I didn't have much choice.

The day was sunny—too sunny for how I felt. The kind of bright sky that made you squint even through sunglasses. On the way, I noticed the gas lines were really long, a mix of different autos fighting for pumps. If they only knew what I was doing there that day.

When I finally pulled into the rest stop, it was under renovation. Half the place was boarded up, and the smell was unforgettable: a mix of diesel fumes, asphalt, and greasy Big Macs from the rooftop smoke stacks. It didn't help my stomach, which already felt like shit.

The detective was waiting by the front door, and he didn't need any introduction. He was a big, burly guy with a face that looked like it had seen everything. The word "detective" might as well have been stitched onto his jacket. I didn't even have to text him that I'd arrived—he locked eyes with me before I was halfway to the door. I was surprised he knew who I was already.

We introduced ourselves and he suggested grabbing something to eat, but I wasn't about to stomach anything. My mouth was dry as a bone, so I settled for a large Coke and hoped it'd help me speak without stammering. The place felt claustrophobic because my head was pounding.

He got straight to it, repeating over and over that this was an active investigation, and he couldn't share much. "The company's under investigation," he said. That's all I got. Gee, thanks, real enlightening.

He started asking about my role in the company, the clients I'd worked with, and whether I knew anything fishy. I told him the truth: I'd left because Rizzo felt shady, and I didn't want any part of it. I shared what little I knew but made it clear I wasn't sure about anything. I really didn't want to be on either side of this crap.

The detective brought up something that made me almost pass out—the Jacob Javits Center event. He asked why I left early that day because he'd been trying to speak with me there. I told him the truth: I left because Rizzo creeped me out. I found it odd that he was there, let alone renting a booth at the event surrounded by his cronies, and it made my skin crawl. None of it made sense to me, and I wanted no part of it.

The detective then mentioned that he'd interrogated Rizzo the week before the event. I had no idea this took place. He called me for phone numbers and shit but left that part out. Rizzo had told him I'd be at the booth with him that day, which was a flat-out lie.

I set the record straight. "That's not true," I said. "I was there to network—hopefully make a few connections— but I was not associated with Rizzo's company any longer." Rizzo was feeding him a line of complete bullshit, and I could tell the detective wasn't buying it anymore.

That's when he reached into his bag and pulled out his cell phone. He pressed play, and there it was: my breakfast conversation. The helmet sitting on the table at the diner wasn't just a weird centerpiece—it was wired for sound. They were cooperating with the DA and recorded the whole meeting and handed it over to the district attorney.

"You're lucky," he said. "You managed to keep yourself clear. Nothing you said at that breakfast tied you to any crime." Lucky? Hearing the word crime for the first time in this whole ordeal didn't feel like luck. It felt like a bad dream I couldn't wake up from.

He told me it looked like I'd just partnered with an asshole, and as far as he could see, I wasn't in trouble.

"The DA will be in touch," he added. "They'll want a full statement from you."

I downed that Diet Coke and left. I was shitting a brick now because it wasn't sitting right with me that I wasn't going to be in any trouble. If you thought I was a mess before, just wait.

By the time I got home, my head was spinning. Sleepless nights followed. I could barely eat, barely think, and I didn't tell Lisa a single word about it. Not one. Every time she asked if I was okay, I just nodded, holding my breath all the while. Come to think of it, I wasn't breathing for months!

Chapter 20

It's a Raid!

No sooner had I left the detective at that rest stop on the NJ Turnpike than my phone buzzed with a call from Rizzo. His voice was frantic, teetering on the edge of panic.

"They just raided my house," he blurted out, barely pausing for breath. "I'm tellin' ya, it was over twenty fuckin' cops. They surrounded my place, swarmed in, and searched everywhere. They took my laptops, all *our* paperwork, and even my cell phone."

For a moment, I couldn't respond. "*This was really happening.*" My mind raced, piecing together what he'd just said. "*Our paperwork?*" That phrase stuck in my head like a thorn. I hadn't been with the company in months, so why was he framing it like we were still a team? I couldn't get the words out of my mouth, but my inner voice was screaming, "*What the fuck do you mean 'our paperwork'?*"

Rizzo's tone shifted slightly as if he realized how exposed he sounded. He added, sheepishly, "They asked about you... and I told 'em you weren't with the company anymore because you had cancer."

I froze. "*Cancer?*" My gut told me this wasn't the cops digging for information about me at this point—it was Rizzo trying to deflect attention from himself by dragging my name into the mix. And now, whether I liked it or not, I was part of the narrative he was spinning. I was pissed.

It was all I could do to keep calm on the phone. Deep breaths, I told myself, trying to slow my racing thoughts. My silence stretched long enough that Rizzo finally asked, "You still there?" I muttered something noncommittal and ended the call, but my mind was far from settled. Whatever Rizzo was caught up in, it was growing, and I had the sinking feeling it wasn't over for me either.

Now the DA had everything. Every shred of paper, every electronic record, every breadcrumb that Rizzo and the company had left behind. They had old records, new records, emails, phone calls, text messages—the works. Names, dates, addresses—it was as if someone had laid my entire professional life bare under the spotlight. I felt exposed in a way I'd never experienced before, like there was no corner to hide in, no crack to slip through.

Doubt crept in, dangerous and relentless. Could I be implicated in this mess? The question gnawed at me, refusing to let go. I replayed every interaction, every email, every meeting with Rizzo, turning them over in my mind like pieces of a puzzle I couldn't solve.

One moment, I'd convince myself I was in the clear. I kept my distance. I walked away. I didn't sign anything shady. But the next moment, a darker thought would creep in. "*What if somethin' slipped through? What if my name's tangled up in ways I can't see?*"

I dissected it all from every angle. "*Was there a message I sent that could be twisted around? A project I touched that might raise questions?*" My mind was like a jury deliberating my own fate, and no matter how many times I argued my innocence, the doubt lingered.

The more I thought about it, the less certain I became. The DA's office had everything—*everything*. What if they found a connection I didn't even know existed? The panic I felt earlier grew heavier, settling like a weight on my chest. Each scenario I played out in my head left me more uncertain than the last, and the line between innocence and implication blurred with every fucking thought.

I had no idea what to do. Fight? Flee? Say nothing? Everything around me seemed to spin, the edges of my vision blurring like I was teetering on the edge of fainting. My heart pounded in my chest, a relentless beating I could hear in my ears. Panic took over, not just in my head but in my entire body. My hands trembled uncontrollably, my legs felt weak, and my breathing turned shallow and rapid, as though I was gasping for air in a room with no oxygen.

This wasn't just anxiety; this was pure, unfiltered terror. Every instinct screamed at me to do something, but I was paralyzed. I couldn't think straight, couldn't focus long enough to plan. The enormity of the situation was suffocating, and for the first time, I realized I wasn't just a bystander to Rizzo's chaos—I was caught in the undertow, being pulled down with him.

Chapter 21

Back at the Ranch

For the longest time, I kept all of this bottled up inside, telling myself I could fix everything if I just got a new business off the ground with a clean slate and a new financial backer. I thought if I focused on moving forward, on rebuilding, I could leave the mess with Rizzo in the past where it belonged. I convinced myself that silence was strength, that I could carry the weight of it all alone. The truth was, I felt the need to keep everything in because I wanted to protect my family and hold onto the hope that there was a way out of the mess without causing them pain. I didn't tell Lisa a single thing, not a hint of what was happening... until Mother's Day.

Mother's Day was sacred in our house, a day we always set aside for Lisa. She had this tradition with me and the boys: every year, we'd go to the local nursery to pick out plants and flowers. Lisa loved creating a bright, welcoming space around our home. Me and the boys would fill the front yard with bursts of color—vibrant marigolds, geraniums, or impatiens—while the backyard always had a touch of wild charm with hydrangeas, eclectic trees, and bushes.

The nursery trips were always a bit much, with the boys putting on their "I'm not bored" faces. Lisa and I had a knack for spotting the best plants and visualizing exactly how they'd look in the yard. Every year, without fail, she'd turn to me with a tray of plants in her hands and say, "This is the year we outdo last year."

By the time we got home, the boys would drag bags of soil and gardening tools to the yard, while Lisa carefully arranged the plants in neat rows, ready for planting. We'd spend hours together digging, planting, and laughing about how messy we all got. The house always looked beautiful afterward, and neighbors would stop to complement our work for weeks. It was one of those simple, perfect traditions that made everything feel normal and steady.

But that year, nothing felt normal. My head wasn't in it, and my chest felt heavy all day. I tried to go along with it, smiling where I could, making small talk with the boys, but my mind was consumed. The weight of what I'd been hiding from Lisa had grown unbearable. I couldn't keep it in anymore.

After we finished planting and were cleaning up in the backyard, I knew I couldn't wait another second. I asked Lisa to sit down on the patio, away from the boys. The sun was beginning to dip in the sky, casting a warm light over the yard. Lisa looked at me, concerned, and she still had her garden gloves on.

And then, I just broke down in tears and let everything out—*everything*. The mess with Rizzo, the investigation, the DA, the raid, the recordings, the healthcare, and money issues—I didn't hold anything back. As I spoke, I felt a mix of emotions: relief from finally being honest but deep sadness knowing I had disappointed her. Lisa had the same expression in her eyes that she had when Tommy was sick. I saw fear, disgust, and dread. Anger was lingering, but not there yet.

When I finished, there was a long, heavy silence between us. The weight of my words hung in the air, and I couldn't even look at her. She managed to ask, "Why didn't you tell me sooner? Do you know how much harder it is for me to hear this now? What are we going to do?" Right then, I had no idea, and I was about to run into a buzzsaw soon.

Lisa has an innate ability to break down complicated situations, and with one sentence, she figures it out. It always pisses me off how she can do that, but that's what I should have done. I should've told her from the start, but I thought I was protecting her. Instead, I'd been shutting her out, leaving her in the dark about something that affected all of us.

She was right, of course. She didn't raise her voice or lash out; that wasn't Lisa's way. But her quiet disappointment stung more than any yelling ever could. How could I lay all this on the person I love the most all in one day—especially on Mother's Day?

I think, at that moment, something shifted in Lisa. It wasn't just anger or frustration; it was like a switch flipped, and she decided she had to take control of the situation. She went into full combat mode with the fierce, unwavering determination she showed when Tommy was diagnosed. Without missing a beat, she declared she was going to make calls to family, friends, and anyone she thought could offer help or guidance. She didn't hesitate, she didn't stop to second-guess herself, and she certainly didn't care about appearances or what anyone might think. As far as Lisa was concerned, this was about survival and straightening out this mess before it spiraled any further.

Her energy was a force of nature I'd seen only a handful of times before. It was clear she wasn't going to let fear or uncertainty paralyze her, and in that moment, I realized that she wasn't just stepping up... she was stepping in. It might have been too late, but Lisa was ready to fight for us, no matter what it took.

While I was lost in my own head, zoning out and trying to make sense of everything, Lisa was on a mission—half-hysterical but determined—trying to explain the situation to anyone who would listen. The problem was, the story was so tangled and complicated, and her frantic delivery didn't make it any easier to follow.

Her family, in their well-meaning but misguided way, decided the best course of action was to email her separation papers. They figured she and the boys would be better off moving back to Staten Island under their care—as if running away could fix everything. Meanwhile, my family, in their infinite wisdom, decided to point the finger at Lisa. They accused her of marrying me for my money—a laughable claim, considering my bank account was running on fumes.

My friends, thankfully, were my saving grace. They didn't need the whole story spelled out; they knew me, knew my character, and stuck by my side. Lisa's family eventually came around, piecing together the truth and realizing this mess wasn't my fault. My family, though? Let's just say they weren't ready to let go of their theory and leave it at that.

As for my friends, they did more than offer moral support. They pulled together a small pool of cash to help keep me afloat for a couple of weeks, proving that real friends show up when it matters. And remember Donato Marchetti, the production manager from Endless Allure Originals? That guy came through in a big way. He lent me his car so I could get around after I had to give one of mine up. I was really losing it by this point.

Chapter 22

Mental Wildfire

The day after the raid on Rizzo's house, an investigator from the district attorney's office called me and wanted to set up an interview in a couple of weeks. Well, I was sure it wasn't for a job opening in their office. The investigator said I could either come in alone or have an attorney present.

I felt nothing but plain fear. The deep, consuming paranoia took hold of me. Everything I did came with a constant need to look over my shoulder. There were moments when it felt utterly unbearable, like I could never truly relax or feel safe. I found myself in a state of perpetual anxiety, my nerves shot and my mind racing. Forget about sleep—I paced the floor every night and had to keep the TV on because the silence drove me nuts. The lack of rest and constant worry caused my appetite to vanish entirely. I wasn't even drinking enough to stay hydrated. My body began to mimic this unraveling. I developed scabs along my hairline, and a peculiar, sour odor seemed to seep from my skin, as if my body itself was reacting to my anxiety.

Whenever I spoke to friends or family face-to-face, I'd leave my phone in the other room, convinced the DA had bugged it. Even though the conversations were mundane, I couldn't shake the feeling that they were listening in, which made me constantly on edge.

At that point, I thought the right move was to start looking for an attorney, and a friend of mine who was a NYC detective gave me the name of a lawyer who was famous for representing mafia guys. His office was in downtown Brooklyn, and I was in no shape to go alone, so I asked my dad to come with me.

Geez, that morning, I was a mess. I was so freakin' distressed. I was positive the cops were about to bust down my door at any second, just like they did with Rizzo, and raid my house. Every little noise or knock on my front door had freaked me out. My mind was racing; I couldn't think straight. So, in a panic, I rushed into my bedroom closet, my heart pounding, and I started grabbing everything I could find. Didn't even stop to think—I just shoved all kinds of papers and documents into two grocery bags like a fucking homeless person.

Here's the sick part: none of that stuff had anything to do with the company or any reason the cops would be after me. My mind was playing tricks, making me see threats that weren't even there. I ended up grabbing a bunch of random, pointless stuff that included old love letters from Lisa, outdated health insurance papers, cell phone bills... total nonsense. I thought I was hiding a huge secret, but really, I was just hauling around personal shit that had nothing to do with anything.

My dad picked me up at the house, and I got in his car, bags in tow, for the trip to Brooklyn for the initial meeting with the attorney. We parked on the other side of Brooklyn to make it easier to find a parking space. We walked to the train station and down into the subway. After a couple of minutes of my father making small talk with me, you can see he was as nervous as I was.

I drifted off by myself to try and gather my thoughts. I stood there on the subway platform, feeling like I was the only person left in the city. The usual noise, the chatter, the rush of people started to fade away—like someone hit the mute button on the world. The platform felt cold, the lights flickered, and a wildfire was brewing in my mind. Time seemed to stop, and the only sound was the screech of the train, getting louder as it came down the tracks.

That sound... it was the only thing cutting through the fog in my head. It felt like a snake slithering through my brain—sharp, relentless, and impossible to ignore. It wasn't just a sound; it was a force that seemed to mess with my inner turmoil. I stepped toward the edge, feeling this strange pull, like something was dragging me closer, telling me to look down at the tracks and not at the train. I couldn't hear a living soul around me. It was like the whole world had shrunk down to just me and that fucking train.

And the pain... God, the pain. I couldn't take it anymore. It felt like I'd been carrying it for so long, and it had finally gotten to be too much. In that moment, I decided I just wanted to jump. I was ready to end it all, to let the train take me and stop everything in my head.

But just as I was about to step off, I felt a hand on my shoulder—firm, but gentle. I turned around, and there was my father, standing there, and his voice broke through all the silence: "Rich, you're standing too close to the edge. Step back. You don't gotta rush. Wait for the train to pull all the way in."

Whether or not my father knew what I was about to do was irrelevant. Those words just broke through. I didn't even realize how far gone I was until he said something. I stepped back, my chest still tight, but starting to loosen a little—like I could breathe again. His hand on my shoulder wasn't just pulling me back literally; it was an anchor, pulling me away from a decision I didn't really want to make. That's all I needed at that moment. I realized I wasn't alone and just needed a kick in the ass.

Chapter 23

Attorneys Out the Wazoo

O n the way to the attorney's office, the silence between us was heavy, like a muggy summer day in the city—except it was still spring. It was just awkward as hell. Neither of us acknowledged what had just happened, like I hadn't tried to jump in front of a train. My dad's always been the silent type, but this was on another level.

By the time we arrived, I'd shoved all my emotions aside. We walked into Joseph Petrocelli and Associates, where the receptionist greeted us with a too-polite smile, the kind meant to make you feel like you're not a criminal. She led me, my dad, and the two shopping bags I was dragging everywhere into his office.

Don't ask me to describe the office—it's a blur. But Petrocelli? He definitely stood out—slick, three-thousand-dollar suit, matching pocket square and tie, and expensive cologne. He looked like the kind of guy who made deals over steak dinners at Sparks without ever having to pick up the bill.

I shook Petrocelli's hand and introduced my father. The first thing he bellowed was, "Your father can't be in the room when you tell me what happened. Anything he hears could be admissible in court." I told him I couldn't do it without my dad there because I was a wreck. Petrocelli just shrugged and said, "It's your funeral. Tell me what happened."

I pulled out a notepad where I'd written everything that happened over the past year and started reading. Before I got far, Petrocelli cut me off, asking for the notepad. The moment I handed it over, he flung it across the room, hitting a potted plant. "Now," he yelled, "tell me in your own words, without the fucking notepad."

So, I did. I rambled on like a machine until he stopped me. "You're an innocent man," he said. "So why are you so upset, and what's with all these fucking bags?" I explained what was in them and told him I agreed I was innocent, but I was being called into the DA's office to share what I knew.

Petrocelli explained that the DA had everything they needed from the Rizzo raid, so I could ditch the bags. He added that they'd want to pull as many people into this shit as possible to build their case and boost their image. Since I used to own the business, he said I'd likely face charges. Then he turned to my father and asked if he'd be willing to put up his house as bail.

My father paused, zoning out for a moment, so I explained what Petrocelli meant. His answer was short: "No, I'm not willing to do that."

Petrocelli pressed him. "Holy fuck, if you don't put up bail, your son, who clearly doesn't have the money, will probably sit in jail until trial and that could take over a year." My father didn't waver. "No, I'm not willing to do that," he repeated.

Hearing my father's answer didn't even affect me because my mind was numb, and at this point, it almost didn't matter what happened to me.

Petrocelli moved on, laying out his fees: a $30,000 retainer to start, more if it went to trial, plus his hourly rate. By then, I wasn't even listening. My mind was stuck on Rikers Island, picturing all the guys lining up to kick the shit out of me while I waited for trial.

I told Petrocelli the money he was asking for was completely out of reach and that I'd go it alone until I could find someone in my price range—which was zero. Without missing a beat, Petrocelli pulled out his phone, hit speed dial, and said, "I'm calling a young attorney in the building I throw cases to sometimes."

He gave me a look that said, "*Hold on a second,*" then spoke to the person on the line, "Hey Johnny, I've got a potential client for you. Can you come down to my office and help him get through a rough patch?" He added he'd try to arrange for him to charge me just $3,000, which would be enough to cover the interview process and see me through until an arrest.

In walked Johnny Valero, my new $3,000 attorney. He was a fun-sized version of Petrocelli. He rocked an expensive suit, jet-black hair—slicked back like Pat Riley in his Knicks glory days, an overstuffed briefcase that looked ready to explode, and, of course, Ferragamo slip-ons.

He launched into his pitch about his clients, how long he'd been doing this, and how he'd be my rock. Did I have a choice? Absolutely not. So, we agreed to terms: he'd show up for the DA interviews with me the following week and, if I got arrested, guide me through that circus.

Chapter 24

Sweating Like a Hooker in Church

The day of the interview, I woke up with a pounding headache, a sore throat, and a nose so clogged it felt like I was breathing through a straw. My temperature read 102—just what I fucking needed. A hot shower barely helped, so I took some flu medicines and started getting ready for this disaster. I picked out a blue blazer but kept fidgeting with it, second-guessing if I was dressed right. No tie—I figured this wasn't formal.

On the train, my mind was spinning. What the fuck was this day going to be like? I had no idea what they'd ask or how it would go down. Then I saw one of my neighbors from Jersey. Oh fuck, no avoiding him. His eyes lit up, and he said, "Hey Rich, where are you headed? New York?" I nodded and said I was going to an interview, which wasn't exactly a lie.

He moved his bag off the seat next to him and talked the whole ride into the city. I can't even remember if I responded. I was too wrapped up in my nerves about the meeting. Thankfully, he got off one stop before mine, giving me a little time to gather my thoughts before meeting Valero.

When I got to the park across from the DA's building, I spotted Valero immediately. He stood out with his Ray-Bans and hair reflecting the sun, legs crossed like he was posing for GQ. I shuffled toward him, wiping my nose with a tissue, trying to ignore the dull ache in my head.

As we walked to the building, Valero gave me quick pointers that sounded rushed and nervous. "Don't extrapolate, just answer the question. If you're unsure, ask to speak to me outside." Normally, I could smell the city when I got off the train, but that day I couldn't smell shit because I was so stuffed up. I felt like one of my senses went on vacation.

As we approached the building, the sun ducked behind its facade, casting a shadow that made the place look even scarier. The revolving doors squeaked as we stepped through, and I just wanted to keep going around instead of exiting. Inside, the hum of the fluorescent lights annoyed me while my head throbbed. I shoved my tissues deeper into my pocket and trudged behind Valero, who swaggered ahead with the kind of confidence only a man with good hair and Ray-Bans can pull off.

Somehow, it felt like half of Manhattan piled into our elevator. Thank God I couldn't smell anything at that point. I'm sure there was a bouquet of aromas wafting off some of the passengers.

The elevator stopped at every floor like it was sightseeing. By the time we reached the 12th floor, I was ready to bail and take the stairs back down.

The doors opened, and it was like walking onto the set of Law and Order. The hallway stretched long and narrow, lined with discolored subway tiles that hadn't been replaced since the 1960s. Every door had one of those wired-glass windows, the kind you'd imagine detectives staring through. Black lettering on each door spelled out the names of the divisions, though the letters were so chipped and faded, they barely mattered. The one door with perfect lettering was the Rackets Division—and that's where we were headed. The site of it cleared my nasal passages for a moment!

At the reception desk, a woman was mid-rant to a co-worker about her boss running her ragged. "I can't even breathe, let alone finish this paperwork," she snapped, waving a folder in his face. "If they don't hire someone soon, I'm quitting." Then she noticed us and her demeanor shifted.

Valero stepped forward and introduced us. "We're here to meet Assistant District Attorney Gerald Thompson," he said.

She replied, "Oh, you're his 9 a.m. meeting. He asked me to bring you to his room, and he'll be right in."

We stepped into the office, and there it was—big as life and twice as horrifying—a PowerPoint projected on the wall. It was a police mafia-like hierarchy chart, and there I was, smack at the top, like I was the boss of this shit. Beneath me, Rizzo, and below him, a lineup of cronies I didn't even recognize. The title of the screen was "The Dead Pool Crew." Real creative bastards. I figured the name came from the dead guy on the permit, but still, talk about a headline that grabs you by the balls.

Before I could fully process it, in walks Thompson. His gray suit hung off him like it was a rental he forgot to get tailored. The office was something else, wall-to-wall stacks of paper so high they doubled as bookshelves for his family photos. The whole place had the kind of disorder you'd expect from someone juggling too many cases at once.

He introduced himself, all polite and apologetic, pretending he had no idea the presentation was still up on the wall. "Sorry about that," he said, rushing to shut it off, but the damage was already done. I didn't catch on at first, but this guy was smooth. Leaving that chart up was no accident. It was a move straight out of a DA's intimidation playbook. And yeah, it worked. I was clammy already—heart racing—and the fever kicked back in. I felt horrible, and this made it ten times worse.

For the first hour, Thompson interviewed me by himself, asking straightforward questions about the business, timelines, and other details. He gave me the usual disclaimer about the investigation being active and how they couldn't share too much, which gave him a lot of leeway with his questioning.

Then the A-Team arrived. The detective I met at the NJ Turnpike rest stop was there, along with two other female detectives from the DA's office. The room was cramped to begin with, but now it was claustrophobic; most of them just leaned against the walls or stacked boxes.

They peppered me with questions for hours, dropping tidbits about what Rizzo had been doing with the money I was owed. They turned the PowerPoint back on, flipping through slides with casual viciousness. One showed Rizzo had been keeping a $6,000-a-month apartment for his girlfriend's use—with the company's money. Another slide highlighted company credit card receipts for strip clubs he frequented in Manhattan. They were trying to get me angry; to make me lose my shit so I'd spill everything they thought I knew. And, motherfucker, it was working. I was furious Rizzo was hiding that chunk of the money from me, living a double life, and tickling strippers in his spare time.

They asked how I managed to survive without a salary. I told them that I hadn't. I'd been robbing Peter to pay Paul through my bank accounts. Thompson spun his computer around, asking if I could show him my accounts. Agitated, I typed in my password, and there they were—my unimpressive bank accounts. Why would I be involved if I didn't stand to gain financially?

Now they shifted into high gear, coming at me tag-team style like the Bosso brothers roughing me up back on 80th Street. One played nice, asking, "What kind of cancer did you have?" while the other barked, "My mother died of cancer—don't use that disease as a prop!"

It felt like whiplash because I was looking at one and then the other. Then they asked if I'd voluntarily hand over my phone to check my texts and calls. Of course, I said yes because I had nothing to hide.

Next thing I know, Detective Harris pulled out a stack of documents from Rizzo's phone records. She started reading text messages between me and Rizzo, zeroing in on why I didn't respond when he made nasty remarks about people.

I flat-out told her, "Because he was crude, and I don't talk about people like that." She thumbed through about a dozen conversations, and I explained them all away. Then Detective Connors jumped in, accusing me of being the brains of the operation. For a split second, I almost felt flattered—no one had ever called me the brains—but then reality hit. I explained that, sure, I'd taught Rizzo the business, but he staffed the projects with unqualified people while I was sick.

Now it was the big detective's turn. He smugly dropped that he was the guy who called me about hiring the phony engineer, the mastermind behind the Javits Center nonsense, and, oh yeah, the genius who wiretapped the motorcycle helmet. Every last person in the room wanted their pound of flesh from me, and they weren't subtle about it. It was like watching a pack of seven-year-olds elbowing each other to be first in line for the Good Humor ice cream truck.

All those times growing up, hearing "Watch your back, kid," a thousand times, and it never sunk in. If someone told me this story about anyone else, I'd roll my eyes and say, "Yeah, serves him right. Should've seen it coming." People will piss on your head and tell you it's raining. But here I was, front and center of my own story, feeling every bit the schmuck.

Finally, Thompson, the good cop the whole time, leaned in with fake sincerity. He told me there was a secret grand jury happening, and I was the only one outside that room who knew about it. Clients were already spilling their guts. He made it clear I wasn't one of the defendants yet, but he was trying to figure out how I fit in. His message was simple: the more I cooperated, the less likely I'd end up on that list of indictments.

Nine hours in, Thompson wrapped it up. "We threw a lot at you today without giving you a clear idea of what we're looking for," he said—like he was my friend. "Now that you have a better understanding, I want you back here next week with more information—something that'll keep you out of prison."

In the meantime, remember my attorney Valero? Yeah, that guy... He was sitting in the back of the room, silent, listening with his pen and pad. I had a feeling he was doodling Looney Tunes characters instead of helping me through the questioning. Every so often, he'd scratch his chin like he was deep in thought or flip a page on his notepad. Meanwhile, I'm sweating bullets, wondering if my attorney had mentally checked out, already planning his next vacation with my quick cash.

I walked out of there completely drained. What started as an interview had turned into an interrogation. My head pounded, my nerves were shot, and I felt like shit. Valero, my so-called rock, sat me on a bench outside before rushing off to his next victim— sorry, client.

I sat there, staring at the sidewalk, and then it hit me all at once. I broke down, sobbing, right there in the street. I thought he'd be there for moral support, even if he hadn't lifted a finger during the DA's barrage.

Valero turned to me, his face all serene, like he just had sex with a prostitute, and said, "You know, isn't Detective Harris hot? As I was sitting there, I know she was giving me the eye."

I froze mid-sob, trying to process what he just said. Is this guy for real? Here I am, crumbling in his lap, my life in his hands, and he's daydreaming about some chick. I stared at him, stunned, as he leaned back like he was picturing her on top of him.

In that moment, I realized Valero wasn't "my rock." Not even close. I wiped my face, shook my head, and stood up to leave. He looked up, confused, like he wanted to ask, "Where are you going?" But I didn't stop and I just kept walking.

Chapter 25

The Wheels Have Fallen Off

If you thought I was a mess before, the week leading up to my next meeting with the DA was dreadful. Somehow, word must've gotten out that I was talking to them because I started getting threats through cryptic texts and phone calls from a burner phone. I felt sick every time my phone buzzed. I was so paranoid I wouldn't let Lisa or the boys leave without me tagging along. If they went to the store, I was right there, thinking I could protect them. It wasn't just for their safety, it was to keep me from spiraling, though it was only a matter of time before that failed.

One afternoon, exhaustion hit, and I crashed on the couch. I must've looked pitiful because Lisa and the boys snuck out to grab lunch. Big mistake. When I woke up, the house was empty, and I was in a cold sweat, heart pounding like a jackhammer. My mind raced through every scenario. Were they safe? Was someone watching them? Watching me? I panicked so much, I

Googled "Life in Prison" on YouTube, thinking that'd help. Spoiler alert: it didn't.

My phone rang. It was Carl Ferraro. He was a bad dude back in the day, or so I'd heard. He worked with us for a bit after straightening his life out, but he was a real piece of work.

His voice sounded like he was going to jump through the phone. "You owe me eight grand," he barked, breathing heavily. "I worked for Rizzo, and that son of a bitch gave me every excuse why my paycheck was late. Now it's time to settle up. I've tried finding him, but he's MIA. I know the town you live in, and I'm headed there now to crack your head open. We can do this the easy way or the hard way."

Carl wasn't exactly a peace-and-love kind of guy. Like E.F. Hutton, when he talked, people listened. My brain was on fire trying to process this when I shot back, "He fucked me too, Carl, and I don't have that kind of money. And besides, I already left the company way before he started screwing you over!"

Carl wasn't buying it. "I don't give a flying fuck," he spat. "Somebody's paying me, and guess what? That somebody's you."

I convinced him to hold off for one more week. I told him the day and time I'd be in the city to meet with the DA. "We'll sort this out then," I added, trying to keep my voice steady. But let's face it, I was thinking about killing two birds with one stone that day... but Carl might have killed me first.

I stumbled into the kitchen, downed an entire 16-ounce carton of orange juice like I was in a Minute Maid commercial, then grabbed rubbing alcohol and poured it on the bottoms of my feet because they were sweating like crazy. I thought it would cool them down. My heart was pounding so loudly I swore I could hear it echoing through the room. It felt like my body was coming apart, like when the Space Shuttle broke up mid-air.

That's when I ran out of the house. I figured fresh air would help, though I'm sure I looked like a lunatic running into the street, clutching my chest. I pulled my cell out and called Lisa, crying, "You gotta come home now! I'm having a heart attack!" Like they didn't have enough to worry about with me already.

While I waited, I figured lying down in the middle of the street was the logical thing to do. I rested my head on the curb, trying to recall my Boy Scout first-aid lessons. The boys had jumped out of the car as it was coming to a stop. I told them to call an ambulance—like it wasn't obvious that their dad sprawled out on the asphalt might need one.

Lisa rode with me in the ambulance while the boys stayed back, waiting for updates. The medic was decent and asked a bunch of questions while he checked my vitals, but all I could focus on was the cost. Healthcare bills were always hanging over my head like a dark cloud.

They wheeled me through the waiting area and got to work fast—tests, scans, and whatever they could run. The first thing they said was I was dehydrated, so they hooked me up to IV fluids. Then the scans came back, that showed something funky with my heart. Great. They needed to keep me overnight for more tests.

Turns out, I was so dehydrated and stressed, my symptoms were mimicking a heart attack. A doctor came in, looked me over, and told me I had something like a nervous breakdown. He must've been psychic. They gave me some meds and sent me on my way.

That night, I crashed on the bed. The week ahead was going to be a shitshow. First thing the next morning, I called Valero to lay out what I needed to talk to the DA about. I gave him a list and made sure he repeated it back to me:

1. I wanted to be a witness on the grand jury. If they just heard my side, I'd walk away from this.
2. I might've watched too many movies, but I needed some type of security or at least info on the Witness Protection Program. The list of

people who wanted to crack my face open was growing.

3. I needed to talk about Ed Lombardo—the mess with him, the money owed, and the fact that my head nearly turned into a home run ball.

Valero wasn't thrilled to hear from me. While on the phone, he brushed off everything I said, poo-pooing all three of my requests. He said he'd ask, but not to hold my breath for answers I'd like.

First, he claimed I couldn't testify to the grand jury for myself—that was off the table. Then he downplayed the threats on my life, saying "It isn't that bad; I have people who don't like me, too." As for Ed Lombardo's Ponzi scheme? He said it had zero impact on my case... don't mention it to the DA because it would just piss him off. Bullshit from Valero... every word of it.

Chapter 26

The Assassins are at it Again

It was time to meet with ADA Thompson and his crew of assassins again. I was feeling better after the flu knocked me out during the last visit, so I hoped for some progress—maybe answers or at least the chance to provide more info. I had prepped, determined to make my case.

But the moment I stepped in, I knew something was off. Thompson's demeanor was colder than last time, irritated before I even said hello. He snapped, "Do you have more info for me? I have other cases and I'm not spending another nine hours with you."

Caught off guard, I think I shit my pants and answered, "I asked Mr. Valero to contact you last week about some questions, and I gave him more info, but he feels it's not relevant."

Thompson's reaction was dismissive. "Well, if your own attorney thinks it's not relevant, you should take his advice. Listen, I'm at the end of this journey with you, and I need answers—real answers."

I didn't have any new bombshells to offer, and I couldn't fake it. Feeling the tension rise, I admitted, "I was scared to come here today. I was hoping you could arrange for some kind of security…"

Thompson cut me off with a loud, mocking laugh. "Sec—Sec—Security? Seriously? We don't provide security. If you didn't hobnob with these people, you wouldn't have to worry about it!"

The room felt smaller with every word. I gathered my courage and asked about testifying before the grand jury, desperate for a chance to speak for myself. But Thompson didn't even look at me when he answered. Instead, he turned to Valero and said, "You're too late. Mr. Valero should've asked me sooner. We're not accepting any other witnesses now." How could I know these things? That's why you have an attorney—to handle this with the DA's office… right?

Frustrated but unable to argue, I sat through the next three hours as Thompson and crew grilled me relentlessly. They pressed me on timelines, clients, and obscure rules and regulations, circling back over and over like they expected me to slip up. By the end, I was mentally and emotionally drained.

Finally, he started gathering the papers on his desk, signaling the end of the meeting. Standing up, he delivered one last ultimatum: "Go home. Give Mr. Valero more information. Something I can actually use and tell him to call me tonight. Otherwise, you'd better be ready to surrender soon."

When I left, Valero stayed behind talking to them for a few minutes. I didn't know who or what about, but when he came out, he had a grin the size of Saskatchewan plastered across his face. "We'll talk outside," he said. "On the park bench." At this point, they should put a plaque on that bench with my name on it—I'd spent enough time there.

Once we sat down, Valero started rambling, practically speaking in tongues about why he hadn't asked Thompson to let me testify before the grand jury or address the issue of security.

I cut him off, shaking my head. "It's done now," I said. "But you need to talk to him about Ed Lombardo. Tell him how I felt threatened the entire time with that guy, why I left, and give him the evidence we have—the stuff that can clear my name."

Valero nodded, his grin finally gone. "I'll call him in an hour and give him everything," he promised.

For the first time in what felt like forever, I exhaled. Maybe I had finally gotten through to them. I hoped I was done with this shitshow. But deep down, I knew better than to let my guard down completely because my luck doesn't usually cooperate.

The next afternoon, around 3:30, he called and said he wasn't getting an answer. He assured me it was nothing unusual, explaining that Thompson's office was overloaded with cases, and they'd get back to him soon.

But something didn't sit right with me. He claimed to be calling Thompson's cell, which was the one Thompson insisted we use to get in touch with him directly. Why wouldn't he pick up when he was so adamant about getting last-ditch info from me?

Over the next few days, I kept reaching out to Valero. Sometimes he answered, sometimes he didn't, and other times he sent a quick text: "Nothing yet." Then, that Friday afternoon, Valero finally called to tell me Detective Harris hadn't returned his calls.

I couldn't believe what I was hearing. "Didn't Thompson say to call him directly?" I asked, my patience wearing thin.

Valero hesitated, sounding confused. "Well, I was calling Harris because she mentioned wanting to grab lunch to discuss the case. I figured she was my point of contact, but she hasn't answered."

I was livid. Without thinking, I flung the phone across the kitchen. But I realized I still needed this asshole, so I picked it back up and snapped, "Call Thompson directly, please, and explain what's been going on... Now!"

I couldn't believe it—my life was on the line, and this guy was more focused on chasing this woman on my dime and letting his peesh do the thinking rather than actually doing his job.

Now I had the whole weekend ahead of me, trying to keep things as normal as possible for Lisa and the boys while stewing over this mess.

As usual, even though Lisa was pressing me for answers, I kept everything close to the vest. My flawed logic told me that if I yelled loud enough, she'd back off and stop asking. In my twisted way, I thought I was protecting her by keeping her in the dark. But let's face it, my strategy sucked.

That weekend was a whirlwind. We argued, we cried, and then we argued some more. We tried to assess the "what ifs" and "how are the boys going to stay in college?" We had so many unanswered questions. This whole mess was out of our control, and yet one thing remained unshakable: Lisa's belief in me.

At a time when my self-confidence was shattered and when I couldn't even muster belief in myself, she kept reassuring me it would work out, even though she had a shadow of doubt. She saw something in me I'd forgotten, and in the chaos of it all, that gave me just enough strength to keep going. I couldn't have made it through the coming weeks without knowing how much she loved me, and it was going to get ugly.

Chapter 27

Cuffs, Prints, and Jail Cells...

OH MY!

I got out of bed early that Monday. I figured I wasn't sleeping anyway, so I might as well keep my mind occupied by doing some yard work. I decided to mow the lawn, hoping the neat stripes I created would take my mind off things for a while.

Mid-stripe, my cell phone rang, shaking me from my thoughts. I answered, holding my breath, and it was Thompson on the other end.

"I'm not supposed to communicate with you directly," he began, his voice sounding irritated. "But your attorney is out of the country on vacation, and he didn't notify my office. Last Friday, I left him a message to have someone available to represent you in case I decided to add you to the indictment. He didn't provide that person."

I could feel my pulse race. "What does that mean?" I asked, trying to keep the panic out of my voice.

"It means," he said matter-of-factly, "I decided to add you to the indictment. You need to report to my office tomorrow at 6 a.m. to surrender. If you don't show up, marshals will come to your house and arrest you. I'm sure that's not how you'd like this to go."

I was so confused but managed to stutter a couple of words like, "Who's gonna be there for..."

He interrupted, his voice sharp. "I will have a public defender in court to represent you. He'll meet you in the courtroom after you're booked. Before the court appearance, he'll tell you how to plead."

I was petrified. This was too much information all at once. I scrambled for words, blurting out the stupidest questions that came to mind. "How do I plead? What should I wear?"

Thompson sighed, clearly annoyed. "Wear your nicest tie," he said sarcastically. "The news outlets will be there."

Yup, this isn't something you think about when living in a quaint town and coaching your son's basketball games at the rec center.

At this point, I checked out mentally. It was the only way my mind was able to deal with this crap. So, I left the lawn half-mowed and went inside to tell Lisa about the call. As I spoke to her in this monotone voice, like I had just had a lobotomy, she broke down. She was a mess—hysterical—and who could blame her? What else do you do when your husband drops this bomb on you?

I can't even explain the rest of the day because it was a blur of trying to figure out what to do next. If Lisa wanted to come to court with me, we didn't have anyone who could step in to take care of Ryan. So, I told her to stay home, and I would call my friend Jimmy to see if he could come with me.

After explaining the situation, I asked, "Hey, Jimmy... I need a favor. Can you meet me at court tomorrow morning at 6 a.m.?" There was no hesitation on his end. "What's the address?" he asked. "I'll be there."

Needless to say, we didn't sleep a wink that night. Lisa spent most of the time on the phone, calling friends and family, desperate for answers or even some reassurance that everything would somehow be okay. She was shaking like a leaf, her voice trembling with every word. I could see the fear in her eyes, and it hurt so badly that I couldn't make her feel better—not yet anyway.

Meanwhile, I sat hunched over on the couch in the family room, staring blankly at the TV. *Everybody Loves*

Raymond was on, but I couldn't hear a single word. Honestly, I should have just muted it because the laughter from the show only made me feel worse—like the rest of the world was fine while our lives were falling apart.

Eventually, I mustered the courage to talk to Frankie and Tommy. I tried to sound calm and collected, doing my best to downplay everything. I made it sound like just another hurdle and an inconvenience rather than the shitstorm that it was. "It's nothing to worry about," I told them, forcing a smile. "We'll get through this."

But their worried eyes told me they didn't believe a word of it. And why would they? They'd already been through so much in their lives. How the fuck could I let this happen? As I looked at them, the guilt was almost unbearable. I could only hope that someday they'd find it in their hearts to forgive me for this mess.

The next morning, I showed up at the park across from the DA's building half an hour early. As I sat on the bench, I thought about how some of the best days of my life were spent frolicking around Manhattan. I was 14 the first time I ventured into the city on my own, tagging along with some friends from Xaverian. We walked from Battery Park all the way to Central Park, and I was absolutely awestruck. I've been hooked on the magic of Manhattan ever since. But today, Manhattan decided it was payback time, and this was going to leave a mark.

I wore a navy blue suit and a striped tie, hoping Thompson would give it the thumbs-up. As I sat there, lost in thought, I spotted Jimmy walking toward me, but his usual grin was nowhere to be found.

Instead, he hugged me, kissed my cheek, and hit me with, "You got this." Ugh, I've always hated that phrase. What do I got? I got nothing but a pounding headache and my life dangling in someone else's hands. So, no, Jimmy, I don't got this!

He leaned in and asked, "You ready to head over there?"

I took a deep breath and shook my head. "No. But let's get this over with."

As we got closer to the building, I caught a whiff of cigarette smoke lingering from someone sitting on another bench. I feel like I can still smell that cigarette today. The sounds of sirens and the subway below added to my growing anxiety.

Normally, I walk through the city at a quick pace, not like a gawking tourist. Not today. Today, I was moving so slowly even a tourist would've yelled at me to pick it up.

Then I saw Rizzo and his crew—seven of them huddled near the entrance like they were getting ready for a game of poker. They were all decked out in tracksuits, each of them with an attorney by their side, briefcases in hand and smug expressions on their faces.

I froze. Panic hit me, and I grabbed Jimmy's arm. "They've got attorneys, Jimmy. And look at all those bastards—they're not even dressed! I'm the only schmuck here in a suit! I look like I'm running this shit!"

Before Jimmy could respond, I yanked off my tie and shoved it into his hands. "Here. Hold this for now." But if you think about it, that wasn't going to help because I still had the suit on!

I planted myself on the other side of the street while they all fixated on me. My palms were clammy, and my heart was racing so fast I'd be surprised if they didn't hear it uptown. I wasn't going anywhere near those guys.

Then the doors to the building flew open for dramatic purposes, and the lead detective stormed out, a bundle of handcuffs jangling in his arms. His voice boomed, "Good morning, gentlemen! Time to be arrested!"

He moved methodically, taking names and cuffing each one of them in a single file. I could feel Jimmy looking at me, but I kept staring straight ahead, or I would have just broken down. The last guy was still muttering something when the detective turned to me and waved me over.

"Let's go. You saw the drill."

My legs felt like lead as I crossed the street. The detective grabbed my hands, turned me around, and zipped the cuffs behind my back. The sound of them closing around my wrists finally echoed the humiliation that washed over me.

Before the doors shut, I glanced back at Jimmy. My voice was barely above a whisper when I managed, "Thank you." It was all I could muster.

We were hauled off to Central Booking, better known as "The Tombs," to be processed—and let me tell you, the name fits. The place looked like something straight out of a horror movie. It was damp and musty; the kind of smell that makes you wonder how long it's been since anyone cared about sanitation. Half the lightbulbs were burned out or flickering, casting eerie shadows on the cracked walls. If you're looking for a "scared straight" experience, an hour in The Tombs would have you walking the straight and narrow for life.

The whole setup was a maze of underground tunnels connecting one building to another. We were shackled together in a line, but I was last, which made me feel a little better. It looked like the first guy in line was the ringleader, and the last guy was the least culpable. Rizzo was first, and seeing him up there helped me stomach being at the tail end.

As we waited to be processed, chaos broke out. A guy from another group, cuffed with his hands behind his back, suddenly made a break for it. I don't know what he thought his plan was, but he took off running down the hallway like a bat out of hell. The cop in charge started yelling, but before he could catch him, the guy lost his balance.

He tripped, and wouldn't you know it, he came flying straight at me. The next thing I knew, we were both on the ground, his full weight pinning me down. His face was inches from mine, and I could feel his hot, sticky breath. Let's just say it wasn't exactly minty fresh. It smelled like the guy hadn't seen the inside of a dentist's office since the Reagan administration.

I gagged, trying to roll him off me, but being cuffed made it almost impossible. The cops swarmed in and hauled him away, but the damage was done. I was left on the floor, humiliated and thoroughly grossed out, wondering if this nightmare could get any worse.

We got back into the elevator and went upstairs for additional processing, shoving each of the tracksuit crew into the holding cell like sardines. When it was finally my turn, I stopped dead in my tracks.

"I'm not going in there," I said firmly.

The detective raised an eyebrow. "What do you mean, you're not going in?"

"I'm not one of them. I'm not going in there."

Something about me struck a nerve with this guy. Maybe it was pity. Maybe he just liked me for some odd reason. Without saying anything, he closed the cell door behind the others and led me into the next room.

There was an old-fashioned radiator against the wall, its chipped paint peeling off. He cuffed me to it and told me, "Stay there, and I'll see what I can do." Stay there? Where was I going? I was cuffed to a radiator. It would have been better if he just said, "I'll be right back," or something... geez.

Minutes stretched into what felt like hours, and I started looking at my hand that wasn't cuffed. It looked green under the fluorescent lights. Can you believe, of all the things I'm thinking about right now, why can't they get decent lighting in these offices?

When he finally came back, he handed me a butter roll and a cup of water for lunch. He said by law they had to feed us, and they usually bought heroes or pizza, but for some reason, we got—a roll.

"Here's the deal," he said, crouching down. "You either go in the cell, or I've gotta send you to Bellevue for a psych eval. That can take days or more. And after that? You'll still have to go through processing anyway. It's your choice. But trust me, you don't wanna go there if you don't have to."

My throat tightened. "Is there anything else we can do?"

"I'll take you back in there and tell them you're sick, so you can't go into the cell," the detective said. "Instead, I'll cuff you to the outside of it."

Then he paused and asked, "Do you need to use the bathroom first?"

I nodded quickly. "Yeah, I do."

He led me to the bathroom, and as soon as the door closed behind us, he turned to me and said, "Now that we're in here alone..."

My mind started racing. "Holy fuck, what's he gonna do to me?"

Sensing my panic, he repeated himself, but his tone softened. "Listen, I've interviewed a lot of your clients and people involved in this case. They all say you're a great guy, that you had nothing to do with any of this. You got caught up in Thompson's hurricane, and once that happens, there's no easy way out."

For a moment, I didn't know what to say... maybe because the smell of urine was stinging my senses. His words meant a lot to me at that moment, but the feeling didn't last once we left the bathroom.

When we got back, they wasted no time prepping us for the walk to the courthouse two blocks away, shackling us together again. Outside, the press was waiting, and it was brutal. Some guys tried to shield their faces with newspapers, but I kept my head down, staring at the ground, thinking back to the cracked concrete in front of my old Brooklyn apartment and playing boxball with my friends.

The photographers shouted and cursed at us, trying to make us look at them for their perfect shot, but I stayed focused on my memory. It was my way of tuning them out. Still, the walk felt endless, and the humiliation was overwhelming. Even now, I can't find a way to joke about it—it's just not there.

The courtroom was draped in that orangish oak— ugly and uninviting. The bailiff crammed members of the press into the jury box, while the overflow spilled into the aisles. He began calling each defendant and their attorney up to the microphone to plead before the judge. One by one, they declared "not guilty," after which the judge would ask Thompson, the prosecutor, to recommend bail. Rizzo and Vincent, who was also in this up to his neck, got slammed with $250,000 bail; others got off with as little as $10,000.

As the judge got closer to calling my name, I felt a tap on my shoulder. Turning, I saw a man with a warm smile who asked, "Are you Richard?"

"Yes," I replied.

"Well, this is your lucky day, Richard. My name is Mark Keller, and I'm your new attorney," he said. "When we get up there, just say 'not guilty,' and we'll talk more after the proceedings."

Sure enough, my name was called. I stood, pled "not guilty," and waited as the judge asked Thompson for my proposed bail. To my surprise, Thompson replied, "No bail is necessary. He has been fully cooperating with my office."

A hush fell over the room. Every eye was on me as I made my way back down the aisle and out of the courtroom. Their fear was palpable. They thought I was cooperating with the DA and wondered what I might have said.

When Keller and I got outside, he let me ramble on and on about what had happened to my original attorney and what I'd already shared with the DA. I spoke for an hour straight, and he didn't interrupt me once. It felt good to have someone to talk to, someone with no skin in the game. Having his ear really helped.

Keller calmly explained the next steps and told me to have patience because it was going to take months to get to the finish line. He gave me assignments to complete and get back to him ASAP, promising to do his best for me.

Exhausted, I got on the train back home. I stared out the window, replaying the whole thing in my mind over and over, thinking of better days. But by the time I got home, the story had hit the news. It was splattered across every New York network and national newspaper. The articles weren't flattering, and neither were the responses from people commenting on them.

When I walked through the door, I looked like I'd spent a week locked in a sauna fully clothed. Lisa greeted me with a big hug and a kiss—her warmth felt so good. She had cooked my favorite dinner, and it was waiting for me: chicken cutlet parmesan and potato pie—my favorites.

The potato pie she makes is a classic Italian casserole with mashed potatoes, butter, mozzarella cheese, and a golden breadcrumb topping. If anything could make you feel better, it was this meal.

Lisa didn't ask about what happened that day, and I certainly wasn't going to talk about it. In fact, I never talked about that day with anyone up to this point. It felt too humiliating to discuss. She needed to see her husband as her rock, and I knew I'd been anything but that. I was more like a piece of Silly Putty.

But I also knew that, like everything else, it would take some time to process. Then it would be time to focus on the work ahead—rebuilding my life and tackling the challenges in front of me.

Chapter 28

The Dresser Drawer Theory

Well, here goes... it was time to push aside the distractions of the gossipers, the finger-pointers, and the endless swirl of blame. I had to focus on what mattered: creating a plan to get my life back on track while managing the court dates looming over me.

I made a list of priorities: find a job, save the house, secure health and life insurance, keep the boys in college, and, of course, tackle the court proceedings.

One of the biggest lessons life has taught me is that trying to handle everything at once is a recipe for failure. We're simply not built to juggle every problem simultaneously—especially when the issues at hand aren't as simple as deciding what color to paint the kitchen.

I think of tackling life's challenges like dealing with a bedroom dresser: if you pull all the drawers open at once, the whole thing will topple over. But if you open one drawer at a time, focus on what's inside that

253

drawer, and close it before moving to the next, everything stays manageable. That's how I decided to face my challenges—one drawer at a time, one problem at a time. It wasn't going to be easy, but it was the only way forward, and besides, who wants to be crushed to death by Pottery Barn furniture?

Navigating the endless cycle of problems was a real grind. One day, I'd be sending out a ton of resumes and calling everyone I knew, asking for a job. The next, I'd be chasing quotes for insurance, and then, like clockwork, I'd find myself on the phone with my attorney, trying to make sense of my case. Every time I turned around, some court date was getting postponed, and each delay felt like my life was still on hold. I just wanted this whole mess to end already, but it felt like it dragged on forever.

Lisa and the boys had faith in me, even on the days when I struggled to find faith in myself. They believed in my strength, my ability to figure things out, and my determination to keep pushing forward no matter what crap was in the way. I knew that if I couldn't find the strength to fight for myself, I had to find it for them. So, I kept opening those drawers, sorting through the shit, and handling whatever I could manage each day. It felt overwhelming, but I had no choice.

One day, I needed to call the business office at Frankie and Tommy's college because both boys had an outstanding balance that needed to be addressed before the year's end. Frankie was about to graduate, and Tommy was preparing for the next academic year. The school informed me that unless these balances were resolved, Frankie wouldn't be allowed to graduate, and Tommy wouldn't be able to register for the following year.

I didn't know what else to do, so I just started talking. I explained to the woman on the other end of the line everything that had been happening in our lives. I told her about the struggles, the stress, and the impossibilities we were facing. I went into so much detail that I didn't even come up for air for a solid ten minutes. When I finally finished, I sat there, holding my breath, unsure of what she might say.

There was a pause, and then the woman spoke. Her voice was calm and filled with kindness. She said, "While you were telling me your story, I opened up a grant the school offers to exceptional students. I reviewed Frankie and Tommy's profiles and considered what I know about them personally. Both boys are extraordinary students and incredible individuals, and they absolutely qualify for this grant. I'm happy to tell you that they're both receiving the grant, and their balances are now completely cleared. Please let them know they don't owe a single penny as far as the school is concerned."

I was stunned. Relief and gratitude washed over me all at once, and I could barely find the words to respond. I thanked her over and over again, up and down, forwards and sideways. I wanted her to know how much her compassion and action meant to me. She was one of those angels who appear in your life just when you need them most.

That day, she didn't just forgive a debt; she gave us hope. In the middle of what felt like an impossible storm, she was the calm. She reminded me that, sometimes, when you open up and share your struggles, people will step forward to help in ways you can never imagine.

DRAWER CLOSED.

Chapter 29

Falling Angels from the Sky

Lisa was relentless, pounding the pavement daily, determined to help me find a job. She reached out to everyone she could think of—acquaintances, former colleagues, even people she barely knew. Social media became the place where she wrote posts about it, but no one was biting.

One afternoon, a friend from town reached out to Lisa, asking if she could do her a favor. The friend needed her hair done for a wedding she and her husband were attending that weekend. Normally, Lisa might have jumped at the chance to help, but that day she felt totally drained, both emotionally and physically. Still, she figured it might be good to distract herself from the stress, so she agreed to help.

She packed up her styling kit, drove over, and was ready to mask her feelings. She forced a smile as she greeted her friend, trying to show the happiness that everyone seemed to expect from her. But midway through the haircut, Lisa's composure began to crumble. Tears trailed down her cheeks, becoming impossible to ignore. Her friend, who was going on and on about the dress she was wearing for the wedding, stopped talking and looked at her in disbelief.

"Lisa, what's wrong?" she asked, her voice filled with concern.

Lisa, always the pillar of strength and resilience, wasn't one to fall apart in front of people. The sight of her struggling was shocking.

Lisa tried to brush it off, shaking her head as if to dismiss the emotion welling up inside her, but the words spilled out before she could stop them. She confessed the frustration, the fear, and the helplessness she felt—not just for herself but for me. All the shit we were going through finally spilled out that night.

The friend listened intently, setting aside her worries about looking fat in the dress and concentrating on Lisa. As they talked, her husband came home from work and strolled into the kitchen, casually asking what was for dinner. Noticing the tension in the room, he quickly realized something more than a usual haircut was happening and stepped out, listening from the family room. Piecing together the conversation, he remembered my line of work from past chats we'd had. He could've easily told himself not to get involved—it wasn't his fucking problem. But he didn't.

Here was a guy who only knew me through a couple of casual conversations and still wanted to help. He went back into the kitchen and asked Lisa for my resume, mentioning that a friend of his had recently launched a similar business. He thought I might be a perfect fit and promised to send it over to see if it could lead to something.

That Monday, I grabbed a stack of my resumes and headed to a hotel in Philly hosting a job fair. The event was crazy with activity, featuring a variety of companies set up in booths, each actively interviewing candidates for open positions. I showed up wearing the same navy suit I used for court appearances—a bad choice in hindsight, but I didn't realize it at the time.

The place was packed, mostly with baby-faced college graduates eager to make some money to pay off their student loans. Lines snaked around the room for each booth, and I found myself about twentieth in line at one. As I waited, I could hear snippets of interviews happening at nearby tables. My ears perked up when a few of the company reps mentioned the salary ranges: $16 to $22 an hour.

That was the moment reality hit me. *"What am I doing here?"* A guy with a family couldn't survive on that.

My stomach churned, and panic started to set in. Without a second thought, I stepped out of the line, got into the elevator, and made my way to the hotel lobby. Finding a quiet corner, I sank into a couch, buried my face in my hands, and just cried hysterically.

The weight of losing the house, failing my family, and running out of options felt unbearable. I kept asking myself out loud, *"How does this all end?"* It felt like there was no way out.

Then, God intervened... and my cell phone rang.

I didn't recognize the number, and with everything going on with my case, I hesitated to answer, thinking it was another threat on my life. Still, something told me to pick up.

"Is this Richie?" the voice on the other end asked. "This is Chris. Our mutual friend Mike sent me your resume, and I'd like to offer you a job."

I had no idea who Mike was for a second, but then I quickly realized it was Lisa's friend's husband who said he would give his friend my resume—one of the angels who stepped into my life without asking for anything in return.

I could hardly believe it. Chris told me a little about the company and outlined the position. They were a really small company that only employed one other person at this point, but it was a manageable salary, had benefits, and, most importantly, offered the lifeline I desperately needed. This was a chance to start over and regain control of my life. In that moment, I knew I had taken a step closer to closing some of the biggest, heaviest drawers in my dresser of worries. Can you believe I got that call at that moment? Yup... I'm crying too!!

I was really doing well with the new job, proving myself and bringing in new business, just like I hadn't skipped a beat since owning my own place. This job was in New Jersey, far removed from the limelight of Manhattan. Most of the people I was dealing with didn't even know what I was going through, which gave me a chance to focus and excel without added judgment.

As my performance continued to impress, I decided it was the right time to tell the owners about my situation. It wasn't an easy decision, and it took a lot of courage because I knew there was a real chance they might let me go. They didn't need to deal with someone bringing extra baggage.

One morning, I mustered up the strength to make the call. As I dialed, my heart felt like it was tickling my

Adam's apple. Chris answered, and before I could lose my balls, I blurted everything out in one breath. He listened carefully and then thanked me for being upfront. He said he appreciated knowing so they wouldn't be blindsided but told me they'd need to discuss it and get back to me.

I braced myself, expecting to wait a couple of nerve-wracking days for their decision. But Chris called me back within half an hour. He told me that he and the other owner, Jeff, had heard so many positive things about me in just the first few weeks that they wanted to keep me on. "Just keep doing what you're doing," he said.

Relief washed over me, and I felt so grateful I wanted to reach through the phone and give him a bear hug. But instead, I played it cool, because sometimes less is more... no?

With that hurdle behind us, Lisa and I could finally turn more of our attention to my case. True to form, Lisa wasted no time getting to work. She began reaching out to friends, family, and anyone who had been part of my life, asking them to write character letters on my behalf to send to the judge.

At first, I wasn't sure how people would respond. It's not exactly easy to ask someone to vouch for you, especially when your life feels like it's under a microscope. But to my surprise, most people were more than happy to help. In fact, they didn't just agree, they poured their hearts into those letters.

Soon, they started rolling in, one after another. More than 60 letters piled up in my living room. I had no idea what to expect but reading them was an experience I'll never forget. Each letter painted a picture of my life through someone else's eyes, and the details they shared overwhelmed me in the best way possible. People wrote about the ways I had helped them, the good I had done, and the impact I had made on their lives. They spoke of my character, my work ethic, my loyalty, and my love for my family.

Every letter felt as if I were being body-surfed through a rock concert, lifted by the strength and support of everyone who believed in me. It was humbling and emotional to realize how many people genuinely cared and wanted to help. Those letters became more than just pieces of paper. They felt like the ending of the movie *It's a Wonderful Life*, a powerful reminder of the lives I had touched and the friends and family who had my back when I needed it most.

Chapter 30

The Angels Have Left the Building

My attorney worked behind the scenes, negotiating with the prosecutor to see if there was a way to get me out of this mess with the least penalty possible. It felt like a game of chess, with me as the piece being moved around the board. They went back and forth, trading offers and counteroffers, while my attorney kept me in the loop. But I couldn't shake the feeling that I was nothing more than a bargaining chip for the prosecutor.

"Richie, they want this, and they will do that for you... Show them that, and they'll take it into consideration." It was a constant push and pull, and no matter how much I cooperated, it never was enough.

What they didn't understand, or didn't care about, was that I had given them everything I could. Everything I knew, I shared. But there were gaps in the puzzle I couldn't fill because I simply wasn't a part of it. That didn't stop them from pressing me, though, as if I were holding back some secret piece of information that would magically help their case.

Court days were the worst. We'd sit in the hallway for hours, waiting for my turn. I'd keep my head down, focusing on the marble tiles beneath my feet, silently counting them over and over. It was easier than looking around and making eye contact with the other defendants. Seeing their faces just made me absolutely sick.

The hallway had these long wooden benches that reminded me of the church pews from my altar boy days. Back then, those pews stood for a place of hope, belonging, and a kind of moral compass I tried to live by. Sitting there in that courthouse hallway felt heavy and made me question if that boy was still inside me.

I couldn't help but let my mind wander back to those days. I remembered the smell of incense filling the church, the prayers bellowing, and the way the stained-glass windows caught the sunlight, casting vibrant colors on people's faces. Back then, I felt proud, standing at the altar, serving in a way that made me feel like I belonged to something bigger than myself.

I wanted to believe that some part of that boy was still there, that I hadn't completely lost the person who took pride in doing the right thing, in being good for the sake of goodness. But sitting there, waiting for my turn in court, it was hard to convince myself. I felt like a stranger to that version of me—a version who just wanted to be liked, to be loved, and to make the people around him proud.

The more I thought about it, the more the questions gnawed at me. Could I ever get back to being that person? Did I even deserve to? The hallway seemed to stretch on endlessly, the sound of voices and footsteps echoing around me, but all I could focus on was the number of tiles beneath my feet and the shadow of my past self.

After all the back-and-forth, my attorney finally delivered the prosecutor's recommendation: they were willing to let me keep my job during the week, but I would have to report to Rikers Island on weekends for three months if I pled guilty. Easy, right? Now all I have to do is agree to this as my plea, and I can just pick daisies on weekends… at Rikers Island.

When he told me this, I absolutely freaked out. The thought of going to Rikers scared the shit out of me. I'd heard the stories about the brutal fights, gang violence, and a level of madness I knew I wasn't built for. I wasn't a pussy by any means, but Rikers? That place could break anyone. I kept imagining the worst-case scenario: getting the piss beaten out of me, losing a piece of myself, and coming out of it as someone I wouldn't even recognize.

As panic set in, I remembered the prosecutor had shared his email address early in the case. Desperate to avoid this nightmare, I took matters into my own hands. Late at night, unable to sleep, I wrote to him, laying out every alternative I could think of—community service, house arrest, even an ankle bracelet—anything to avoid Rikers. I poured my heart into those emails, hoping to find a solution that wouldn't destroy me.

Each email went unanswered, and I felt increasingly helpless. Once you're in the system, the odds are stacked against you. They hold all the cards, forcing you to take a plea because the cost of clearing your name at trial is insurmountable. It's ridiculous, but it's the reality.

After what felt like an eternity of endless court dates, judgment day finally arrived. It was the moment everything had been building toward, the day that would decide our future. Lisa and I took the train into the city that morning, both of us lost in our own thoughts. The ride was quiet, each of us trying to mentally prepare for what lay ahead.

When we got off the train, we decided to walk a few blocks before we got to the courthouse. It wasn't far, but it felt like miles. I think we were both trying to cling to some semblance of normalcy, as if strolling hand-in-hand through the city streets could make this just another day.

The summer heat was the kind that makes the pavement look wavy, blurring everything in the distance like a mirage... and I could only hope that's what this all was. As we walked, our hands were locked together, fingers intertwined, but it didn't feel like our usual bond. Our palms were sweating, yet neither of us let go. It was as if holding on to each other might change the outcome of the case.

Lisa squeezed my hand occasionally, her way of telling me she was there, that we were in this together. We turned the corner, and there was the courthouse, just waiting for us. I could feel my heart pounding as we approached, and my anxiety was through the roof. The walk hadn't made me feel normal, but it had given me a moment to hold on to Lisa, to draw strength from her before we went in.

As we moved through the metal detectors, the courthouse was in full swing—the guards barking instructions, and a line of people emptying their pockets. Just as I placed my belt in the plastic bin, I spotted Thompson, the prosecutor, walking confidently toward the elevators. His badge flashed, and he bypassed the metal detectors. I guess that's a privilege, and it exhibited the distance between us.

Before I could even react, Lisa, ignoring every rule or protocol, ran around the side of a barricade. She was determined to speak to Thompson.

"Lisa, no," I started to say, but it was too late.

"Excuse me, Mr. Thompson," she called out, her pitch changing to her battlefield voice.

Thompson stopped mid-stride and turned, his face briefly showing some surprise before settling back into his professional demeanor.

"We've done all our talking with your husband's attorney," he said curtly, his tone very dismissive. "Nothing you say to me now will have any bearing on the outcome."

He turned slightly, ready to walk away, but Lisa wasn't finished.

With tears now streaming down her face, she stepped closer, undeterred by his coldness. "You've destroyed a good man," she said, her voice trembling. "A man who had no part in this. How can you be so callous? You should have listened with your heart, not with your ego. It seems like you didn't take anything he told you into account through this whole thing."

Her words rang through the hallway, drawing everyone's attention. For a moment, it looked like Thompson lost his composure. His expression softened slightly, and it was as if he wanted to say something to explain or justify himself but, instead, he turned back toward the elevator. It looked like his jaw tightened. He stepped inside, the doors sliding shut, leaving Lisa standing there, her shoulders visibly shaking as she fought to hold herself together.

I knew Lisa well enough to understand she wasn't looking for a response from Thompson. She just needed to tell him how she felt. That's my girl. You could see she'd already received what she needed. That crack in his face told her everything—deep down, it seemed he couldn't shake the lingering doubt that he might not be doing the right thing.

Chapter 31

To Plea or Not to Plea

The courtroom was buzzing with activity, a blend of tension and anticipation. Reporters lined the back wall along with their cameramen. When I sat down, I could feel their eyes penetrating the back of my head. Families of defendants in cases ahead of us sat together, whispering nervously or staring blankly ahead, lost in their own thoughts. And then there was Lisa and me, seated quietly in a corner, trying to shrink into the background while bracing for what was to come.

We had deliberately chosen not to bring Frankie, Tommy, and Ryan to these sessions, especially this one. The attorney had suggested otherwise, arguing it might show the court a more human side of a devoted father with a family who loved and depended on him. While it made sense legally, as a father, it felt unthinkable.

Lisa and I discussed it, weighing the potential benefits against the emotional toll. The thought of my boys in that courtroom was unbearable. This wasn't just another chapter in my story, it would become part of theirs, a memory I didn't want them to carry.

Frankie and Tommy were old enough to understand, but as Lisa put it, "How do you explain this to them later? How do you make them unsee it?" Ryan, only eight at the time, wasn't even a consideration.

This was no longer about me. It was about protecting them from this reality. The courtroom wasn't a place for them, so we decided against it, even if it cost us a legal advantage. I didn't want them to see me like this—a man in court, waiting for his fate.

"All rise!" the bailiff bellowed, his voice echoing through the courtroom. As everyone stood, it sounded like a screeching car in my head. My stomach churned, but I kept my eyes forward, focusing on the judge's bench, hoping he just wouldn't show up.

My attorney motioned for me to join him at the front of the room. I turned to Lisa, who was gripping my hand so fucking tight... as if letting go might make me disappear. Her eyes were filled with tears, but she forced a brave smile, and I leaned in to give her one last kiss. It was quick, but it signified everything we couldn't say aloud in that moment.

Her fingers wouldn't let go of mine, but eventually, I had to pull away. As I slinked up to the second row to take my place beside my attorney, I felt so bad that I was putting her through this. Sliding into the hard wooden seat, I exhaled slowly, trying to collect myself.

"This is it," I thought, glancing around the room. My attorney leaned in, whispering something meant to reassure me, but I barely heard him. My focus was already shifting to the judge, who actually did show up and settled into his chair.

I tried to sit up straight, wiped my damp palms on my pants, and braced myself for what was coming next. I heard my own breath and was simply grateful to still have it. The bailiff called my name, signaling that I was next on the docket. I sat in the front row with my attorney. This was the first time in my life that front-row tickets truly sucked.

The charges were read aloud, and my stomach churned as names of people and addresses of projects I'd never even heard of echoed through the courtroom. I leaned toward my attorney, whispering, "I don't know these people or places."

He shot back, "You've already accepted the plea. When the judge asks how you plead, just say guilty."

The list of charges came to an end, and the judge's voice boomed, "How do you plead?"

I froze. My chest tightened, and before I could stop myself, I completely broke down right there in the front row. It wasn't a whimper, it was a full-on sob—like I was an Italian grandmother mourning at her son's funeral.

"I need a moment with my attorney," I choked out.

The judge, visibly irritated, granted a 15-minute recess.

Out in the lobby, my attorney's frustration spilled out. "What the heck are you doing?" he said, all pissed off. "You got a good deal!"

I wiped my face, still trembling. "I can't do it. I don't know those people or those buildings. I didn't do this, and I can't plead guilty."

His tone softened slightly. "This is the deal you made. You have to stick to it. Be strong. You'll be alright."

Lisa stepped in closer. She didn't say a word, but the look on her face carried all the reassurance I needed. It was her silent way of saying, "You've got this. You'll be okay."

I took a deep breath, tried to gather any strength I had left, and we headed back inside. As we walked through the doors, I noticed Thompson at the bench, engaged in a sidebar with the judge. The judge didn't look happy. His lips moved in a mutter I couldn't make out, and Thompson's face was uncharacteristically somber.

I was a mess. My face burned, my eyes were swollen, and my nose was running uncontrollably. The judge glanced at me with an expression that was both annoyed and oddly empathetic. Then, something I never expected happened: instead of asking us to stand, he gestured for us to remain seated.

The judge turned his full attention to me. "Mr. Thompson tells me you cooperated fully," he began. "In light of this and other things he told me, the plea deal is being walked back. You are free to go." Then he slammed the gavel onto the desk, and the crack of it might have been the sweetest sound I'd ever heard. No jail time, no probation, and I was walking out of there a free man.

For a moment, I didn't process the words. Free? Just like that? I sat there, stunned, trying to grasp what he'd just said. I stood slowly, feeling like I was walking through a dream, and made my way toward Lisa, who was waiting by the door. Her face lit up with relief, but I could tell she wanted to get out of there as fast as possible, scared shitless that they might change their minds.

Before we left, I had one last thing to do. I approached Thompson, who was packing up his briefcase. "I appreciate what you did," I said, as I tried to keep my voice steady. "But now that you've ruined my career, what am I supposed to do?"

He paused, looking at me with an expression I couldn't quite read. "You're a good man," he said quietly. "People really like you. You'll be fine."

With that, I walked away, feeling both numb and relieved. I was free to go, but was I truly free? News articles, rumors, and whispers would follow me everywhere. Still, as Lisa grabbed my hand and we walked away from that courthouse together, I felt a spark of hope. It was surreal, but for the first time in a long while, I dared to believe we'd find a way forward, as more dresser drawers were finally closing for good.

Chapter 32

A Life of Rainbows and Unicorns

When we got home from court, I stepped straight into the shower, letting the hot water almost burn my skin, as if I could wash away every ounce of that experience. When I finally got out, I threw on a pair of shorts and a t-shirt and headed straight for my closet. I began rummaging through all the clothes I'd worn to court over those grueling months—the suits, ties, shirts, and shoes that felt like a uniform for the worst chapter of my life. One by one, I yanked them off the hangers, piling them into my arms until I could barely carry them.

On my way down the stairs, I passed Lisa, who was on the phone with her sister. She paused, holding her hand over the receiver. "What are you doing with all those clothes?" she asked, giving me a confused look.

"I'm taking them to the yard to burn them," I said nonchalantly, like I burned clothes daily or something.

"I don't even want to donate them because they're bad luck now, and I'm fucking done with them."

Lisa just watched, shaking her head, but she didn't stop me. I headed to the yard, dumped the pile into the fire pit, and soaked it with lighter fluid. Then, I tossed the match and set it all ablaze.

The flames grew, and as the smoke rose, I didn't just feel relief from the physical act of burning those clothes. Mentally, it was the real purge I needed. Watching it all turn to ash was like shedding a skin I never wanted to wear again. That fire wasn't just burning suits; it was burning the weight of those months, giving me a chance to start fresh.

As for the other defendants in the case? They all received some jail time, but Rizzo, being the big fish, faced the harshest penalty—three years behind bars and nearly $750,000 in restitution.

Oh, and remember the first chapter of the book with the guy Lombardo and his brother? The Securities and Exchange Commission finally caught up with them too. They were slapped with two years in prison and a staggering $3,000,000 in restitution. All these guys made my life miserable, but justice finally caught up with them. They had practically flaunted their schemes in front of the Department of Buildings and the SEC, which, in response, implemented sweeping changes to their divisions.

Fast forward a few years, and I'm flipping through *The New York Post.* I get to page four, and the headline hits me: "Prosecutor Resigns After Allegedly Withholding Evidence." I kept reading, and sure enough, it's Thompson.

I knew it all along! My gut had told me during my case that evidence was being withheld—or at the very least, slow-dripped to ensure it couldn't be admissible. Seeing that article brought all the anxiety back and pissed me off all over again. I eventually let it go, trusting that God has His own way of handling things, and it seems God handled things for Thompson. The last I heard, he was living in West Virginia, working as a defense attorney. West Virginia?? Maybe he is representing coal miners out there... who knows.

And back to Rizzo, well, he was true to form. After serving his time, he somehow managed to get in trouble again for the same scheme that landed him in prison the first time. Shame on the city for allowing him to practice again. Who's really at fault for letting him shyster people out of their money once more?

As for me? Let's just say rainbows aren't exclusive to pride parades—they're also powerful symbols of hope and resilience. I dug deep, opened those last couple of drawers, and not only managed to save the house by bargaining with the bank but also helped our marriage grow stronger than ever. Together, we weathered every storm, and the boys flourished in ways that continue to amaze me. Frankie earned his PhD in epidemiology, Tommy achieved a double master's in business, and Ryan is well on his way to becoming a star on stage and screen.

The family has grown since those days. We now have daughters-in-law and grandchildren, filling our lives with even more joy and purpose. Lisa and I aren't perfect parents, but we do our best and hope that love, care, and effort shine through.

We thrived despite facing what felt like insurmountable obstacles—sickness, financial struggles, and legal battles. For some families, it might have been a recipe for disaster, but for us, it was proof of the strength love can bring to any situation.

Sure, not everyone stuck around. Some family members drifted away, choosing their own truths and paths. And you know what? That's okay. I've learned that you can still love someone, even if they've hurt you deeply—you just love them in a unique way and from a distance.

In the end, life is about perseverance, faith, and leaning into the connections that matter most. For us, those challenges didn't break us; they forged something unshakable.

After a bit of hard work, the company owners rewarded me with the role of Director of Operations. Together, we grew the business from a small team of three to a thriving organization with over seventy employees. They believed in me, I believed in them, and it turned out to be a win for everyone.

As I look back on my eventful life, I often reflect on the dreams I thought were important. But life kept throwing shit in my way. For years, I poured my energy into chasing success, believing it was defined by money, status, and the shiny trinkets that came with it.

Today, my definition of success couldn't be more different. It has evolved with every fistfight I had as a kid, each weird situation I got myself into, and even the triumphs. Success, as I see it now, is not about money, fancy cars, or living in the best house on the block. Don't get me wrong—who still wouldn't want that? But they pale in comparison to the joy of a long walk with Lisa, sharing a Diet Coke during a drive to our son's house, or lying in bed on a quiet morning and talking about nothing at all. It's also time spent with our kids and grandkids that fills my heart. Times like these make me one of the richest people in the world.

A friend of Lisa's once said something that stuck with me: "Richie won't be judged by what happened to him but by how he overcame those challenges and emerged stronger." That's been a guiding truth for me. It's not about avoiding hardships but rising from them.

You'd think that after everything I've experienced, fought for, and survived in my life, I'd have been much smarter. How could I have fallen for this bullshit? I've made my share of mistakes—more than I'd like to admit. But falling prey to a shyster? I should have seen it coming a mile away. My problem was I had too much to handle at that point in my life, and I should have sat back and thought a little bit more instead of reacting.

Life has shown me we're not designed to juggle every problem simultaneously. Naturally, dresser drawers still need to be opened and closed in my life, but I'll be smarter about it and take my time to figure out which one needs to be handled at the time.

Some of these situations were self-created, and some I comically fell into. Whether it was stepping into spots where I should have called the police or thinking I could tough out my own acute mental health struggles, I often believed I could bear it all. Life has taught me that sometimes, you need help. There's no shame in seeking support—whether from friends and family or from an actual professional. It's not a sign of weakness; it's a sign of growth.

And then there are the little things that bring me complete joy—the small details that add meaning to everyday life. For instance, why can't I find a decent landscaper? After firing more than a few so-called professionals, I decided to take care of the lawn myself these past few years. It's not about saving money; it's about knowing the job's done right.

I love the satisfaction that nobody can do it the way I can. Whether it's a lawn or a burger, when my hands are on the work, it's done with care, precision, and a little bit of swagger. It reminds me of my first job at Burger King, carefully placing the pickles on a Whopper. When I do it, it's perfect, no matter how long it fucking takes!